INTERNET
TRAFFIC & LEADS

INTERNET TRAFFIC & LEADS

THE PAST, PRESENT AND FUTURE OF INTERNET MARKETING FOR ENTREPRENEURS WHO WANT TO WIN

Vince Reed

ISBN: 1534738010
ISBN 13: 9781534738010

TABLE OF CONTENTS

FORWARD
By: Jeff Moore – President Of International Pacific Seafoods and Founder Of Thursday Night Boardroom

A s we travel through our lives, there are people that inspire, motivate and fuel us to be better than we are today. We vicariously share their successes, we feel their setbacks and we quietly celebrate how they persevere… and ultimately come to the conclusion that anything is possible if we clearly set our intentions, focus on the process and dedicate our energy to making something great.

I am fortunate to have a wonderful family with an amazing wife and four fabulous children. They inspire me and make me want to be a better father, husband and man every day.

I am abundantly blessed to also have a group of friends that compel me to raise the bar in my business, my personal life and the way that I serve.

There is one man, a dear friend, a confidant, an advisor that I can always look to in order to test the outer limits of my capacity; a friend that stretches his limits and breaks through to new heights almost as naturally as other people simply stroll through life.

This man is Vince Reed.

As the president International Pacific Seafoods, an 8-Figure seafood company, founder of Thursday Night Boardroom, a global entrepreneurial and marketing mastermind group with chapters across the USA and over 500 members from 24 countries and the co-host of The Deep Dive Podcast, I get a chance to meet and work with some of the most extraordinary people in the world.

Vince Reed is among the most forward thinking, intelligent, hardworking and thoughtful people I have ever met. And when it comes to driving targeted traffic and leads to businesses and creating compelling offers that people are eager to buy, both online and offline, Vince has no peer.

To say that Vince continues to reinvent himself constantly and consistently is a major understatement. I met Vince when he walked through the door at Thursday Night Boardroom in mid-2011. At that time, Vince had an online training company called Net Divvy, where he taught home based entrepreneurs, Network and Multi-Level Marketers how to escape the "Friends & Family" model of building their businesses by using the power of the internet to build massive downlines... as Vince had done himself several times. Vince is and always has been a guy that plays by the Learn – Do – Teach model of business.

When we met, Vince was making in the mid to high 5 figures a month. He was on a constant mission to create a 7-figure business and was testing new models almost monthly.

Vince has always been a hard worker that was willing to follow the blueprint to success. From the time he was in high school as a leading college football prospect with poor grades, who worked his butt off his senior year and successfully earned a Division 1 scholarship by following the exact instructions and guidance from his counselor (side note: That high school counselor was and is my wife), to the time he learned that all he had to do was make more calls than anyone at his mortgage company in order to crush previous records and earn piles of money in his early twenties. Vince was more than willing to put in the work, he was EAGER.

In 2013, Vince had an epiphany. It seems almost cliché, but Vince went from focusing on earning 7-figures to purely focusing on helping others build their 7-figure businesses.

Serving... and providing enormous value on a consistent basis was his 100% focus. He created systems and processes that when followed, would help any serious entrepreneur create massive prosperity as long as they were willing to put in the work. His success system was so effective and predictable that he could map out a person's entrepreneurial journey and even their revenue with 100% certainty.

My Internet Traffic System (MITS for short), the integrated suite of products and programs, and his Internet Traffic Live event were products of his epiphany.

Vince's Secret Sauce is really no secret at all; an insatiable curiosity, an absolute disbelief that "good enough" is NEVER good enough, and the unconditional belief that he will out hustle and out work anyone is really his entire formula.

Being Vince's friend, or as he calls me, his "Secret Weapon" (again, not much of a secret) is no simple task. There are late night calls with simple but powerful business models coupled with complex multi-tiered funnels he tries to explain (on the phone) while I am half asleep, to the text messages summoning me to his home up the street to review his White Board, to his last minute requests to review copy or even come up with a compelling headline are the price of admission to the back stage experience that is Vince's ever evolving mind.

In this book, you are going to get a more vivid glimpse of this man who has become one of the most sought after traffic and conversion specialists in the world today.

This book is going to reveal Vince's journey from humble beginnings as a newbie internet and network marketer earning mid 5-figures a month, to a major league thought leader, online media juggernaut and business building change agent earning more in a month than most Fortune 500 executives earn in a year.

And throughout these pages, he is going to give you the map to follow so you can create your own journey to prosperity and abundance.

Fasten your seatbelt; you are in for an awesome ride.

Jeff L Moore
President – International Pacific Seafoods
Founder – Thursday Night Boardroom
www.ThursdayNightBoardroom.com
jmoore@internationalpacific.com

INTRODUCTION
The Red Bugatti And The $60,000 A Week Effect

Daily life for most people is incredibly mundane! Days are filled with the same old routine of waking up, guzzling down a gallon of coffee just to get a jolt and jump-start before slogging through *another monotonous 24 hours.*

Another boring day of the tedious 9-5 grind! Another day of mindless TV watching! Another day gone by with your dreams being one step closer to the grave.

And then it happens…

You walk outside one morning as you're strolling along on the way to your 97' Honda Accord.

And out of nowhere it appears! You hear its roar getting louder and louder the closer it speeds towards you. You hear its beastly purr as it effortlessly shifts gears and gains speed. The leaves begin to rustle and fight one another in the street as if a thunderous storm is heading your way!

Then, lightning past you is a Cherry Red, Bugatti Veyron. Pure luxury. A supercar packed with over 1,000 horsepower and can go from 0-60 in 2.7 seconds. It's. a. BEAST!

You'd swear its driver grinned and winked at you, like it's some sort of sign, but you can't be sure as the moment happened so fast.

This experience cranks up some excitement into your soul as the Bugatti breezes past you and disappears into the horizon. You nearly give yourself *whiplash* as you spin your head around. This thing's got 100% of your attention! Because it's not just another car. **It's REMARKABLE.**

This is what I call "The Bugatti" effect.

Many experience a similar effect when I tell them they can be making $60,000 a week in their online business. They just don't see how that's possible, yet.

But believe me, it's totally possible for you! And you picking up this book and beginning to read it is a great first step in the right direction.

I don't mean to sound arrogant, but I've done it over and over and over again. I've built THREE separate 7-figure businesses by using the exact success formulas found within this book, which you're now privy to!

As countless thousands are spinning their wheels just trying to make a buck online, my students and I are quietly making millions. And it's because we understand that it's all about simple systems and knowing simple numbers. That's it!

Just as a finely tuned vehicle like a Bugatti needs its eight-liter, 16-cylinder turbocharged engine, and the premium fuel to make it purr like a big cat, likewise, in order to get to say, $60,000 a week and up, you need the right types of Traffic and Leads to make your profits purr.

And you need simple formulas you can follow, which will speed you into the promised land of profits, making you a rip-roaring success!

Here's just a *small preview* of what you'll discover as you race through this book…

You'll clearly see how you can get:

> 1,000 leads at $3.00 a click (easy)
> 30% to show up to a webinar (simple)
> 10% to buy a $997 Product or Service
> 2X sales by follow-up and webinar replay
> (Rinse & Repeat)
> Now you've got a $60,000/week business!

This is a simple breakdown of just one formula you're now holding in your hands! Of course, there are nuances and specific things you must do to pull this off. Yet, this hopefully demonstrates to you the power of knowing your numbers, and then being confident you know exactly how to hit those numbers.

All the formulas for you to do that are in this book! All of my secrets have been revealed. And I'm so excited to be passing them on to you! They've changed my life from one of being broke and stressed, to now touching the lives of countless individuals and making myself a literal fortune, doing what I love in the process.

Now, it's your turn.

It's time to create the "Bugatti Effect" in your life. Implement what you learn in this book, soak in the nuggets of wisdom as you're reading my story, believe in yourself and stay consistent, and you'll experience neck-breaking, head-turning results as you never have before!

That's my personal guarantee to you.

Are you ready to put the key in the ignition and start?

Vroom Vroom.

To your success,
Vince Reed

Vince Reed – Internet Traffic – The Past, The
Present, And The Future For Entrepreneurs
Who Want To Use The Internet To Win

CHAPTER 1

My Story

My name is Vince Reed and I should be dead. I've always told myself that if I were to write a book, I would start it off this way. I spent the early years of my life living in the inner city of Los Angeles. Gang activity was rampant. The frequent sounds of gunshots thundering through the streets as I lie in bed trying to go to sleep. I know that some people watch movies like Boyz N The Hood, Menace II Society, or Training Day and they wonder if that is how things really are. In some ways, Hollywood can embellish the truth. Honestly though, from what I can remember being there, it's much worse than what most would think.

I will never forget the day walking home from school at seven years old with my sister. As we sped our little feet across the concrete jungle to get home, a group of girls came out of nowhere. Like feral cats. Claws out. Ready to feast on us. They jumped her and started trying to beat her up. And she would cry out to me, "Vince, go hide in the bushes and wait for me!" This happened often; nearly every week it would. I would not even cry or be too afraid, because she would actually end up beating all of them up by herself! Then we would just continue walking home like nothing even happened.

My sister was a fighter. And her protective instinct was fierce.

Me on the other hand? I'm no thug. Certainly, I'm no gangster! And thankfully, I've never done time or veered down that path. My struggles took a different route. I had moved to the suburbs with my dad at seven years old and lived a normal middle to upper class life. Although my dad was a very successful executive who taught me lessons every day, he always made it clear about how things would be growing up. "I have money. You have nothing." He would tell me. I always knew that I would have to earn my keep in my home! There would be no spoiling me. No living off of daddy.

You may be wondering why then I should be dead.

I should be dead because I was born prematurely. After being in the womb for just seven months, I was ready for the whole wide world! My birth weight was just 3lbs 4 ounces. I've eaten hamburgers nearly that big! The doctors kept me in intensive care for over one month, until I could reach a healthy weight. There was a real fear that I would not make it. To the point where they moved me to another hospital several miles away from my mother, who was also bedridden after the birth for a few weeks.

The word is that my dad would have to travel back and forth between hospitals. Over to one to feed me, and then over to the other to be with my mother. This explains the unbreakable bond that I have with my father, even to this day.

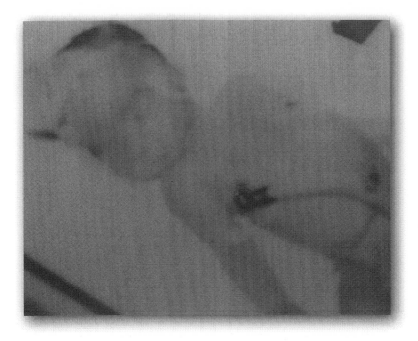

I remember seeing my picture with a lot of tubes and gad-
gets of all sorts attached to me, just to keep me alive. I was so
small that I could literally fit into the palm of my father's hand.
Today, I'm 6'1" and am at a healthy weight of 195lbs.

The good news from all of this is that I survived. My life
could have ended before it had even begun. I feel so fortunate to be here at 4am in the morning as I sit here writing this
book for you. I've always been an impatient person, so that
probably explains why I couldn't wait two more months to be
born! I know I get the impatient trait from my Dad. It's this
trait that allows me to get things done. It's the reason I set a
goal for myself to complete this book in seven days and not
even blink about it, knowing with full confidence that I would
get it done.

Here's a few steps I took:

Step 1 – Buy a few books on how to write a book.

Step 2 - Listen to the audio version on warp speed.

Step 3 - Take notes on my phone on what I need to do.

Step 4 – Set a goal to write the book in one week.

If I can write two chapters a day, then boom, I'm done. And I know that the knowledge and lessons learned that I share will absolutely transform lives.

Considering the fact that my mother is an author, it gave me a nudge towards this calling to write a book. She's my inspiration. Because up until later in her life, she was actually illiterate. To see her educate herself and write several books always amazed me. She loved proving people wrong! There is no doubt I have that same trait grafted deep into my bones. And that comes from her. She showed me that nothing and nobody can stop a person that has the determination and will to go after what they want in life.

Thank you mom and dad for all you have done for me.

Now that you know I am not a gun slinging thug, and I do have parents that have guided me along the way, let's move on to the good stuff. The reason you have invested in this book.

I love online marketing even more than I loved playing sports growing up. I went to the University of Colorado on a football scholarship and had dreams all my life of playing in the

NFL. I thought I could be the next Marcus Allan. That's why I wore the number 32!

Yet, I can honestly say that my passion for online marketing is much greater than it is for sports.

I believe it's greater because unless you are playing a sport like tennis, most sports are team sports. If you master the internet though and you work towards mastery, you can be the Michael Jordan of your industry. Even if you can't slam dunk from the free throw line. And even if you can't throw a football like Tom Brady, don't worry about it. Because when it comes to the Internet, when you commit to mastery, you can be the Tom Brady or Michael Jordan of your field. And you can do it from anywhere in the world, despite your background or experience. You only need to commit to being committed!

I love internet marketing because I truly believe absolutely anyone can master it and use it to make a lot of money. And more importantly, you can use it to impact a lot of people. After all, making an impact is really what life is all about!

When I was getting started and was learning how to use the internet, I knew I was going to be a millionaire. There was zero doubt about that. And you should be confident of that too if you are reading this book right now. I still believe that the internet is untapped territory. And if you take what I share with you to heart and put it into action, you will have all the tools necessary to succeed in business and in life.

I include your life here because I will be giving you quite a few life stories and will be sharing experiences that will not only help you in your business, but life as well. Some of the lessons you will read in this book will help you in your wealth, your relationships, and with your overall health. If your relationships and health are not solid, trust me, your business will eventually crumble! And, you won't be happy. I want you to be rich and happy!

Groundhog Day With Dad
If you have ever seen the movie Groundhog Day with Bill Murray, you will understand why I call this portion of the book Groundhog Day.

The movie consists of Bill Murray reliving the same day over and over again. You remember his alarm going off every morning right? The same thing, every morning. The alarm starts to beep. And then it's Sonny and Cher singing, "I Got You, Babe" in the background as the DJ says, "Okay campers, rise and shine. And don't forget your booties because it's cold out there today!"

Well, when I moved with my dad at seven years old, I felt that my life was like that movie.

My dad had consistently coached me in sports. From the time I was eight years old, all the way until I was a freshman in high school. Every. Single. Day. He would tell me stories as he drove to practice. He would tell me stories as we ate dinner. And, he would tell me stories as I lie in the bed sleeping. Well, maybe not when I was sleeping, but it sure felt like it! And oftentimes, I'd listen to his stories and they'd be the last thing of the day that I'd hear as my eyes drew heavy, and I began to doze off to sleep.

He would also make sure to ask me questions along with his stories.

Let me take you inside just one of these car rides home:

Dad: When I was in college, one time I was with a group of friends. And they went into this liquor store and stole a bunch of stuff. When they came back out, I refused to get into the car with them. I told them to take it all back into the store, or I would not be leaving with them in that car. They called me a punk and all kinds of other names that would make the average man comply. I didn't get in and they left me. Stranded all alone. As I stood there watching them drive off, nearly as soon as they pulled out of the lot I heard the sirens go off. Just around the corner they got pulled over and all of them were arrested. I would have been too if I'd been in that car.

You see son, I am a leader. Not a follower. Are you listening to me?

Me: Yes, dad.

Dad: Are you a leader or a follower, son?

Me: I'm a leader, dad.

Dad: If people try to make you do drugs, what are you going to say?

Me: No.

Dad: When they call you a punk and make fun of you, what are you going to say or do?

Me: I'd walk away.

Dad: Why?

Me: Because, I'm a leader, not a follower. Just like you.

Now if you can imagine every day from the time you were seven years old, added in with countless other stories until the time you are 14 years old, you would understand why I am the way I am today.

This is a million dollar lesson in business and in life.

If you want to be successful, you must be willing to go left when everyone else is going right, and vice versa. Zig when they zag. When they go for a hook, deliver a massive uppercut to rock and shock them all.

When it comes to business, I realized very early on that if no one was aware of my business, then I would not be profitable. It's like having a McDonalds in the middle of the dessert that no one knows exists. I didn't want to be the business out by itself in the middle of the desert. So I knew lead generation would be integral to my overall success. I also realized the best thing of all! The thing that made me very excited. The fact that I didn't need to go to school for 25 years - maybe a slight exaggeration - like a doctor or lawyer must so that I could become wealthy. All I needed to do was commit to mastery.

Needless to say, I was sold on mastering the internet from that moment forward!

With just a few hours a day you could learn enough to build a business that attracts dream customers to you, instead of you relentlessly hunting them down, hoping and desperately praying that they buy something from you.

My Love Fest With The Internet
I never did make it into the NFL. In fact, I barely even saw the field in college. In high school I was the man! In college, I was just another role player on the team. A pawn in a violent game of Chess. It didn't take long for me to realize that my dream of playing football on Sundays in the NFL was not going to happen. No Super Bowl Sunday experience for me, except

by sitting on the couch like everyone else, Doritos and Beer in hand.

I would have these dreams often of my dad telling me, "I have money. You have nothing."

This meant that after college, I was going to have do *something* with my life. So I put all of my energy into my studies. And I quickly became a Buff Scholar at the University of Colorado, which is an award given to athletes who achieve a 3.4 or higher GPA.

I graduated college early and went back home to California. I remember my dad cut me off after only one week of being home. He told me to go out there and make it happen! So, I left, and went back to Los Angeles to live with my brother.

There I spent the first few months depressed as I watched many of my friends and both of my college roommates live out their dreams in the NFL. One of them actually played so well that he started in the Pro Bowl.

After putting down the Sony PlayStation, the Cookies, and Doritos which had me balloon up to 220 pounds, I finally found a job working at ING Direct as a banker. Sounds like big bucks, right? This was during the very beginning of the Real Estate boom. I got the job and they paid me a whopping $24,000 a year. I thought I was going to be rich, believe it or not. That is until I got my first check and half of it was gone! What was going on?!

I went and showed my brother as if ING had made a huge mistake. My brother looked at me, and laughed one of those deep in your belly laughs, and then he said, "TAXES, dude."

As he walked away still laughing at me, my ego steadily declining, he yelled, "Welcome to the REAL world!"

Sadly, today my brother is no longer with me. He died unexpectedly. Words can't express my love for him and the things he taught me and did for me. He made a man out of me! And he is actually the reason I'm an internet marketer today, resulting in millions being made. This is because he always had his own online businesses. When my real estate career ended, I know that my openness to explore opportunities on the internet was solely because of him. Thank You brother.

As I sit here writing this right now thinking of my brother, tears are beginning to well up inside of me. So, let's move on...

When I worked at ING, the Real Estate industry was absolute bananas. The volume of inbound calls was unreal! Every stinking banker had this fancy head set on. We would not even have to pick up and answer the phone. It would just B-E-E-P, and a person would be on the line. When that person hung up the phone, it would go off again, B-E-E-P, and another person would be on the line. This would happen over and over again throughout my entire shift. All day long, B-E-E-P. I can't even tell you how many calls I took everyday.

When people would call, my job was to do one of two things. If they had a home mortgage I was to sell them on a saving account, which was paying a whopping 1.5%. That interest rate would be amazing if you could still get that today! If they had a saving account, a mortgage, or were looking for a home, I was to offer them a lower rate mortgage or a new home loan.

I remember having between 20 to 50 million dollars in loan applications submitted every week. Because I was just the person taking the applications though, I did not get paid on any of that which I didn't have a clue about at the time but would soon find out about.

After I stopped looking for Uncle Sam -the government withholding taxes- to ask him to give me half of my paycheck back, I started working overtime only to see good old Uncle Sam steal even more. This was my first lesson about the limitation of being a wage earner and the benefits of being an entrepreneur. The last straw was when I asked my manager how much he made, and he told me $35,000 per year, plus bonuses.

I asked him how long he had been working there, and he said seven years. And immediately, I knew that this rat race was not for me. I'm not opposed to hard work by any means, but the way Uncle Sam would take my hard-earned money, coupled with the fact that I had no solid path to financial freedom where I was at, I knew this was not for me right then and there. Times would be a changing.

The Dinner That Changed It All

One day, I got a call from my cousin and he invited me to go to dinner with him. At dinner he told me he made $12,000 that month doing loans working for a small broker firm. I remember thinking it would take me 12 months to earn what he earned in just one month after taxes! Let's just say that my ears became very attentive. Like a hungry fox honed in to the sounds of a mouse scurrying in the leaves nearby, he had my full attention.

He asked me what I was doing at ING. After I explained what I was doing, he informed me that the applications that I take go straight to a loan officer who will make 3% or more on every loan they submit.

This was before smart phones, so I wrote on a piece of paper 20 million x 3% and then I almost fell out of my chair. I realized that someone was earning up to $600,000 a week processing the loans *I* was taking applications for. And they were paying me a measly $24,000 a year. Wow. Can someone say, exit plan?

He then said, "You should come work for us Vince! We are a small broker, and you will get a small base plus benefits, and you will kill it." He said that I could charge my own fees and that they have people earning $30,000 per month working with them. I said, "Sign me up now!" He set up an interview for me and the next day I quit my job at ING after only working there for four months. Sayonara fellas.

I remember going in for the interview to the new job and they said, "Yes, you can work here, but your start date would be in two weeks." I said, "Awesome! But do you mind if I come in and work for free for the next two weeks so that I can learn? And when I do start I can be off and running from day one?" They said, "Sure!" "I have one more question," I said. "If I write 20 million in loans will that give me 3% no matter what?" They looked at me, smiled, and said, "Yes, you will kid! In fact, you could get as much as 6% depending on the deal." Clearly no one was writing that much business in the office. But that was exactly what I had been doing when I was taking applications every day at ING.

This all meant that I had some things to do, and fast.

I had to move back home from Los Angeles to Orange County with my dad and stepmom whom I never got along with. I was broke and had only $600 to my name. I had not started working at my new job yet, so I had no guaranteed money coming in. After moving back home with my dad, within 48 hours my stepmom and I got into a huge argument. Apparently my clothes were not good enough for the closet. She told me I had to put my clothes in the garage, instead of being able to use the space in the closet in my brother's old room where their clothes that had not been worn or moved for years hung. So I asked why I couldn't move their unused clothes to the garage and put my clothes in the closet? She told me absolutely not, we got into a huge argument, and I ended up moving out.

So I packed my things up. All of my possessions were just my clothes, the $600 to my name, a small TV with a VCR built into it and my air mattress. I gathered it all up and left quite angrily.

I drove to Irvine, California where my job was to see if I could find a place there to live.

I believe that God was looking out for me, because I saw a sign for this apartment that said I could get 1 ½ months free with a 12 month lease and only a $300 deposit! I went into the leasing office, and I remember the building was still under construction. A few minutes later, I walked out with a new one-bedroom apartment for $300 and I didn't have to pay rent for 45 days.

I was literally the first tenant in the building! It was a luxury apartment in Irvine, California. Today, those same one bed-room apartments rent for over $3,000. My rent back then was $1,500, which for me felt like a million dollars at the time.

I was freaked out and this decision was really stressful but it was either this or sleep in my car. The apartment sounded good.

I hadn't officially started the job yet. Which meant I needed to make money fast!

I remember when I moved in, I didn't have enough money for a bed or couches or nearly any basic necessities, so I set my air mattress up on the floor in the living room and borrowed VHS movies to watch on my little TV from friends. I could not even afford cable or a phone, and that little TV was the size of a laptop computer at best. My family had no idea where I was. And I wasn't sure I wanted to tell them. The first two nights there I literally cried myself to sleep. Laying there on the floor, in this nice, but cold and barren apartment. All alone in the world.

That Monday, I went to the office to start working, again before I was even considered an actual employee. But I wanted to get a head start on it all. I met my manager and I remember telling him to not let me be average and that I wanted to be the best there.

He told me that if I'd make more phone calls than anyone else, then I would be more successful than anyone else. I then asked him if I could work weekends, and he said, "You have a key to the office now, work as much as you want."

The absolute first thing I did was go around and ask all of the loan officers if they had old leads that they did not want. Every one of them opened a drawer on their desk, rustled around a bit, and then handed me stacks of old leads. Ones they had deemed unworthy. They only liked calling the fresh leads that the company handed out to them, piping hot, daily.

By the end of the first day my desk was covered with stacks of leads! The clock was ticking. I was down to my last $200 after a couple bad late night food decisions. So I decided to stock up on cereal and peanut butter and jelly to last me for the next two months.

The advantage I had over everyone else was the fact that I was used to talking on the phone nonstop because of my experience at ING. I couldn't understand why everyone was just sitting around talking all day, waiting for fresh leads or money to magically fall from the sky. They just weren't hungry like I was. I had the eye of the tiger!

So I went home, and devised an action plan that I would 100% execute on. I would get to the office early, I would stay later than everyone else, and I would work weekends while everyone else was out playing and blowing all of their money.

I got an unexplainable rush from being there working when the nightlights came on in the office, and the cleaning people were coming in late, wiping down desks and throwing away trash. And there I was, hustling.

By my official first day of work, I had seven loans submitted in my pipeline from leads that other people in the office didn't want. Those leads that they had deemed duds turned into gold, and I closed my first deal during my 1st official week of working there. I got my paycheck 30 days later, just one week before my rent was due. The check was for $6,746 and I thought I was Donald Trump, baby!

I went and bought couches for the living room. I invested in some more Captain Crunch and PB & J. And I moved my air mattress into the bedroom. I was just like the Jefferson's. Moving on up.

My next check was for over $17,000. I thereafter went and bought a bed and some clothes and became one of the top producers in the company by my third month working there. My hustle was working. Always remember to hustle. To work harder and smarter than everyone else.

Yep. Hard work got me by then. It gets me by today. And it will for you too. It can make you a millionaire! I'm living and breathing proof of that.

I went on to have a very productive career in Real Estate for a while. However, when the big bubble burst, the internet found me, and I thank God every day that it did.

CHAPTER 2

BUILDING A BUSINESS IS LIKE GOING TO SCHOOL ALL OVER AGAIN - HOW THIS BOOK IS LAID OUT

I f I were to tell you that the worst day of my life would actually turn out to be the best day of my life, you would think I'm nuts. Yet, it's absolutely true.

It was the summer of 2007. At this point, I had started and already closed my mortgage company. Then I was asked by a broker friend of mine to come back and do FHA loans for him. Although I never got a FHA deal to fund, as you will learn here in a moment, at the time they were supposedly the only loans that were getting approved. When I went back to do these loans I was flat broke. My home was in pre-foreclosure. And I was extremely depressed to the point where I was playing online poker, and racking up credit card debt while trying to get rich quick!

A couple weeks into doing loans again I had submitted eight loans. Many of my customers were telling me that other brokers could not get the loans to go through for them. So they were elated when they heard that I was able to make it work for them!

All of their files came back from the bank as clean approvals. I remember thinking, "I'm back, baby!" After it was all said and done, if these deals were to fund, I would clear over $50,000, just like that. It was just what I would need in order to save my home and get out of debt.

The day before all of the loans were scheduled to be signed, I went home and I was so excited. I walked through the doors feeling like a man again. I went in to talk to my girlfriend -now my wife- about it all, and I ensured her that things were about to get much better for us as soon as these deals went through. For a good while she had been the one that was paying all of the bills, buying the food, and keeping me mentally strong. It felt good that I would be able to bring something to the table again! She was very happy for me. For us.

As I was driving to the office the next day, I didn't feel very well. I felt like something wasn't quite right. I walked into my office, sat down at my desk, and turned on my computer. I went straight to my email to see when the notary was going to go out so I could sign the documents. And that's when I saw it in my inbox. It was staring directly at me. It felt like the grim reaper had come to take my soul.

The subject line read: SORRY

I didn't even need to open up the email to know what was coming next.

The message went on to say, "Sorry, but all eight of your loans will not be going to docs today. At this time we must seize funding until further notice. Please notify your clients. Thanks and have a good day." Really?!

My heart nearly fell out of my chest. And all I could think about was, "How am I going to tell my girlfriend?" I remember thinking, "She won't want to stay with me. Is she going to think I'm a loser?"

Even worse, I was thinking how I was going to tell the bad news to all of the people who were also depending on these deals to go through in order to save their homes. I called them all, one depressing call at a time to tell them what had happened. It seemed that each call got worse and worse. I was cursed and yelled at. I'm sure if I were delivering the news in person, I would have been spat on. And there were even a few racial slurs that came my way. I brushed it all off and tried my best to take it like a man.

I remember packing up all of my files and tossing them in my bag that day. I was preparing myself to go back home and face my girlfriend. Yet, *something* told me to wait!

Something told me to go online and find a job, right then and there. I did not want to go home with that type of bad news without at least trying to look for something else to do first!

So I went to the only place I knew of at the time to find a job. Craigslist. I went straight to the sales section, and I saw an ad that said, "Make Money on GOOGLE." "Hmm... Interesting!" I thought. It was smack dab in the middle of the page and it stood out like a sore thumb!

"Make Money on GOOGLE," sounded a lot better than asking customers if they wanted fries with their order.

I was not a computer literate person at the time. I could barely even send an attachment in an email. But I clicked on the ad anyways, and there was this lady saying how she had made millions on the internet.

I checked her out, and she seemed legit. So I took down her number, grabbed my bag, and left the office. I didn't even tell my boss I wasn't coming back, because I was afraid he would try to talk me into staying. And I was done!

On the short yet very long drive home, as afraid as I was of what was to come next, the fact that I was going to lose my home, the fact that the following week my lease was up on my car and I was going to lose that too, I still had this sweet little feeling well up inside of me.

As bad as everything was, I remember being very excited about this Internet thing. The thought of being an Internet millionaire actually came across my mind at that moment. I had that lovely feeling you get when you buy a lottery ticket and the Powerball goes up to $100 million.

You know, that feeling of "*what-if?!*"

I pull into my driveway, walk inside the door to my home, and my girlfriend stands there with this incredibly happy and expectant look on her face. As if she were expecting me to trot in and start dancing around the house screaming, "I'm back!"

That smile quickly turned to a look of a woman who was deeply concerned and grieved. As I told her what happened, she lovingly and patiently listened to me. Then I broke the *best news* of the night to her. "Don't worry BABE," I said. "I found something else that I'm going to do!"

She said, "What are you going to do Vince?!"

I said, and I quote, "I'm going to make money on Google!"

The look on her face could have made me rich right then and there. Priceless.

As her jaw dropped to the floor, I said to her, "Babe, I was on Craigslist today and there was this lady who said she's made millions on Google. And she wants to teach me how she did it!"

As I write this, I can't help but laugh at myself for how ridiculous this must have sounded to her.

I will never forget the look on her face as she tried to hold back the tears. You don't forget those looks. Ever. She took a deep breath, gathered her composure, and said to me, "Well, at least go do some research on it babe!"

And that is exactly what I did. That was the moment the Internet found me! That is the reason you are reading this book. And that is the reason I can scream from the top of the mountain today:

"I'm a #$%!ing Internet Millionaire!"

Well, without the curse word of course.

I will be forever grateful for my girlfriend, whom is now my beautiful wife. I love you babe. Thanks for always believing in me! Had you told me I was crazy at that moment, it is possible I would not have pursued the Internet as a career.

That is how the worst day of my life became the best day of my life. Because it was the day that internet marketing found me.

How This Book Is Laid Out

The reason I say the Internet found me is because as I started researching different companies on Google, per my girlfriend's recommendation, and I started to see all of the various paid ads, I started to put small pieces of the puzzle together. I called the millionaire lady from Craigslist, and honestly, I just didn't get a good vibe from her.

So I continued to do research, I found something interesting, and I decided to send $2,000 that I got from selling items of mine on Craigslist, believe it or not, to a complete stranger that I had met online. He was a top earner in his company. I signed up with his team, and I claimed my spot in this direct sales company. I decided to join him because no matter where I seemed to search online for different direct sales companies, his ads would always show up!

I said to myself, "There has to be other people like me looking for ways to make money! If I could just learn how to do what he is doing, I will be rich too!"

Now that I was on his team, I remember calling him and I asked, "Can you teach me how you are placing those ads on Google?" And he said, "Yes Vince, I can!" He briefly explained the concept of it all to me. You pick a targeted keyword, and when a person searches for that keyword, your ad pops up and boom, you're rich. With NO training and NO guidance, I did what most beginners do. I jumped in and blew money I didn't have. Mainly because I was not patient enough to learn the strategies behind the advertising first. So I gathered up $1,000 that I didn't have, transferred it to my Google Ads account, and I quickly went on to lose that $1,000 in under 30 minutes. Ouch. That hurt.

That's when I knew this internet thing was not going to be like an easy walk in the park on a beautiful spring day.

However, I was determined not to quit! I saw a glimmer of light at the end of the tunnel!

Although I did not make a single dime with that direct sales company, sending him $2,000 was like me paying my tuition for my freshman year of internet marketing school. After I lost the $1,000, I called him up and asked him if he had anymore training I could watch, so I could learn how to run my ads "just a little" better. That's when he led me to my first mentor and now good friend, Jonathan Budd. At the time, he was the hottest and most popular online marketer within the home business industry. His mentoring gave me an incredible education that aided in my eventual success online. The things I learned over the next 90 to 120 days on the internet was mind-blowing and worth every penny I have invested.

As you continue to read this book, I will lay everything out for you as if you are going through each year of college, entering into grad school, and going off into the real world. The truth of the matter is; I was lucky enough to be able to attend college on a full ride football scholarship. For most people, college can easily cost several hundred thousand dollars. In a similar manner, you must be willing to invest in yourself and your entrepreneurial education. Like me, you'll find it to be worth every penny that you've invested.

The internet is not easy, my friend. In fact, it took me six months just to make a single commission. Yet looking back, now I realize that I was simply a freshman in Internet Marketing College. I was just beginning to learn the ropes.

Just to get by, I sold nearly every possession in my home. I borrowed some money from my lesson-telling father, and I got lucky as I stumbled onto an account that I had forgot I even had. Remember those stories I told you about that my father would tell me? One story he also told me was this:

"Never spend your last dollar, son. Ever."

Well, when things were going good in Real Estate, I had a financial advisor come to my office. And he had set me up with an account that took $500 from my bank account every month. Because I was not opening up my mail because of all the bills, the fear of even looking at what I owed and confronting my situation, I never even noticed the statements from that financial institution that was holding my money. When my girlfriend sorted through the pile of mail one day, she opened a letter up and realized I had over $10,000 sitting there in that account! So what do you think I did with that money?

You're darn right! I took it out and invested it into my business. And I splurged a little bit on us too.

Finally, I was able to take my girlfriend out to a dinner that she didn't have to pay for! I felt a little bit like a man again.

Now that you know things were not easy for me to get where I am today, let's just say that once I made that first commission, things started to change rapidly. My 1st commission was for a whopping $6.70. After I saw that commission email come in, it was like something clicked with me. And the commissions started to come in much faster. I was beginning to get very excited.

As time went on commission emails became an every week thing, then an every day thing and soon an every hour thing. Today my inbox is flooded with commissions emails almost by the minute. I know it sounds crazy but I want you to know and believe what's possible!

I very quickly became the number one distributor in this new Network Marketing company I joined, which led to my very first six figure year online. Put your seat belts on folks. Because this story is going to shift into training mode now. Full speed ahead! I'll reveal powerful stories and secrets to you, experiences discovered through the streets of hard knocks, all which will take you deep inside my mind and that will teach you everything you need to know about making money and generating targeted leads online. I will unearth to you incredible marketing strategies and selling techniques that will make you wildly profitable from the internet. My goal is to make sure that you don't have to go through all of the same frustrating and time wasting ups and downs that I went through back when I got my start. Strap in. Things are about to get very interesting.

CHAPTER 3

FRESHMAN YEAR – WALKING 10 MILES IN THE SNOW - WHAT TO DO WHEN YOU GET A LEAD

Growing up, I would hear stories from my parents and family friends about how much easier "us kids" have it compared to them. On occasion, you would hear a crazy story about how they had to walk 10 miles, each way, through a blizzard, just to get to school or work, or somewhere. I remember rolling my eyes. Of course, I get what they were saying now that I am older myself!

When I got started in my online business, there were no books like the one you're holding in your hands right now. There was nothing showing you a clear cut way to become successful. When information products were created to teach these strategies, they were a minimum of one-thousand to two-thousand dollars each. And the gurus would create products on every topic under the sun! If you wanted to learn it? You had to buy it.

Then to take things further, you had to figure out exactly how you could make their system work for your specific business model. And finally, if you wanted the guru's more personalized help, you would soon be out tens of thousands of dollars more!

I had always come up with a way to invest in their products because I knew I needed that information if I were to become successful. That's age old advice, right? Seek out the individuals who are getting the results that you desire, and simply model what they are doing. My advice to you is this. Even though you may not have invested thousands to buy this book, the information contained within it is worth millions. It's priceless, really. Take this book seriously, and finish it. This is your life we're talking about here! Massive change and results will come to you only if you're ready to accept it. So commit to not letting this be another half read book on your shelf. Take in the knowledge. And then, *apply* the knowledge. Because knowledge is not power. *Applied* knowledge is.

I would have never even known that this internet world existed had it not been for that original ad that I came across on Craigslist. And more importantly, eventually stumbling upon the network marketing industry.

Funny as it sounds, I got my start as an online marketer because of network marketing. I didn't want to chase friends and pester all of my relatives to check out what I was doing as most people are instructed to do. So learning how to generate my own qualified leads online seemed like the logical thing for me to be doing. To this day, I still don't understand why traditional network marketers chase non-entrepreneurs like their friends and family, to join their businesses.

Here's the truth. I know a lot of entrepreneurs and small business owners look down on the network marketing industry. I've talked to hundreds of entrepreneurs out there, and when I tell them that's where I got my start? Well, they stare at me with a look of confusion and near disgust on their faces. Then they say, "You mean one of those pyramid things?!"

For those of you who don't view network marketing as a good business model, what I will tell you is that it can be a great educational platform for people who want to start a business. It can help you develop some grit, and learn the basic skills essential for success in any business venture. Because of network marketing, my phone now has more millionaires on speed dial than Donald Trump has! Well, probably not more than Trump has, but I'm getting there!

As my good friend and blogging mentor, Ray Higdon, who by the way happens to have earned eight figures between his network marketing business, his information marketing business, and his coaching business says, "People don't have a problem with network marketing, they have a problem with *network marketers.*"

I could not agree with him more. Instead of selling the products, most network marketers tend to focus on only recruiting. This is why building a network marketing business is not easy for most people! The myth or story that is often told to distributors is that if you get two people, and then they get two, then you will be rich. It's ridiculous. It's as crazy as the local restaurant owner basing their success on customers going out and getting two people to come eat!

That is why when I got started, I never focused on recruiting. I focused on the *solution* that my products solved. I then focused on *eliminating the pain* that the newest distributors were constantly experiencing.

Most new distributors I've found really struggle with having the appropriate amount of business capital they need to really succeed. And nearly 100% of them will struggle with getting consistent, quality leads.

This is why my goal and mission was to get them paid as fast as possible. To show them how they could generate their own leads daily. And most importantly, I wanted to reveal to them my proven process that would ensure they were successful. So I focused on *simulating* what it would feel like if they were actually hired for a new job, and were going through the two-week training process with me.

I found out that most entrepreneurs don't have a problem with working hard or learning how to build a business. What they have a problem with is learning everything they need to know and then putting in the hours to be successful, and here's the kicker, without a *guaranteed paycheck*.

This is because they are used to trading dollars for time. Working 40 hours a week for example, knowing their company will pay them X dollars as agreed upon. They do the work. They get paid. But that's not being an entrepreneur. That's being a wage slave. In writing this book, every morning I've been getting up at 4AM. Just me, the sunrise, and a cup of green tea. No distractions. No boss looking over my shoulders to hold me accountable. I get focused, and I write until 8 or 9

INTERNET TRAFFIC & LEADS

in the morning. This was done with zero guarantee of future earnings. I'm not promised to earn one red cent from all of this hard work. However, I focus on the *value,* and I know with certainty that the money will come as a result.

The amount of money you make is in direct correlation to the amount of value that you offer to the world!

Focus not on the result, or the dollars per hour earned. But rather focus on the daily, consistent activities that will get you to the result. Take care of that and provide the value to your marketplace, and the results and big bucks will come, trust me. Me and my rich pals have the bank statements to back that statement up, 100%.

All of this plays hand in hand with you really knowing your customers.

The best entrepreneurs in the world understand their customers better than the customers even understand themselves! That is true power. They also provide more value than all of their competitors do.

In today's society most people are programed at a young age to go to school so they can get a good job, work for two weeks and get a paycheck in return. When you start your own business? It is a completely different culture. Totally opposite!

You could work for months on end, and in my case six months before you see a single dime in return. All the while, you are spending money that you don't have to get you to where you need to be. You're taking step after step after step, yet it doesn't look like you are getting anywhere.

That is why I call this portion of the book, "Walking 10 Miles in the Snow!"

Everything you do when you first start out in your business is you paying your dues! It's you learning the ropes, and it's you putting in your 10,000 hours of hard work. Which according to Malcolm Gladwell in his groundbreaking book, The Tipping Point, states 10,000 hours is the time you must put in to be an expert in any given field or niche. Now this does not mean that you can't earn while you learn. Yet, it does mean that it takes time to become truly Pro. Be willing to slog through the snow as long as it takes. Put in your 10 miles!

Success was not easy for me. But eventually, I was able to crack the network marketing code because I was able to merge it with the internet.

After learning how to create a basic sales funnel and some basic lead generation strategies, I created a system that allowed me to become the #1 distributor in my company within 6 months.

The organization that I built was 90% of the company and it grew to well over 20,000 distributors! I eventually created a training website that the company endorsed as their official training website.

I started doing training webinars for the entire company. And over time I built a list up to over 25,000 people that I could continue to advertise to, for life.

So now you may be wondering, how did I do it?

First off, it was not easy. I experienced a *lot* of pain along the way. The good news is that building businesses now is very easy for me. And it can be for you too! Once you learn these principles you can rinse and repeat over and over again and get very positive results, every single time. In fact, if you learn from your prior mistakes each time, you can get even better results than you did before you had made them. Mistakes can prove to be very profitable ventures! Yes, failing your way forward is one of the very best success strategies out there!

What I'm about to share with you next will work for *any* business, if you implement these same principles.

There are 2 things I want you to always remember if you want to earn more money in a single day than most people earn in a month or even a year.

1. The key to being successful in business is to allow your advertising to run 24/7/365. This means that you must always be putting your message in front of the right people at all times. Wouldn't it be great if you had a team of the best salesmen in the world working for you around the clock, every single day of the year including holidays?! Later in the book, I will talk to you about targeting the right type of customers. It will be the secret sauce that will give you the edge you need over your competitors.

2. You must have a process that you take every lead through which educates them about you and your business. You must give them certainty and confidence that they can be successful. And last but not least, you must have a simple system that allows them to get started fast.

Some of you may be saying, "How can I afford to advertise 24/7/365?" And, "How can I develop such a process to take my leads through?"

We'll be addressing both of these questions in the book. We will dive deep together into the secrets of scaling your marketing even if you have a small budget. We'll discuss all of this in the book, in detail. First things first though. Right now, we need to address how you should be creating a basic sales funnel.

Think of a traditional, literal funnel that you could pour water into the top of, and a small portion of what you poured into the top comes out of the bottom. That is what a proper sales funnel will do for your business. It filters out all the dirt allowing you to find the diamonds. When you combine the power of a good sales funnel with targeted leads flowing through it regularly, you instantly have a profitable business on your hands.

Once you start learning how to generate your own leads, there are four key things you must get across to your potential customers or leads. I normally would make a four-part video series, which I would send to my leads immediately after they enter their information into my website or capture page. A capture page, just so you know, is basically a single page website with a headline and/or video that asks for a person's email address, in exchange for you giving them valuable information. There's usually no other links or buttons that they can click on. It's hyper-focused. They can either put in their email address for more information, or they can click off of the site. Video is very powerful right now, so I most often leverage it in my pages.

Below is what each video would say:

Video 1: Who Am I?

In this video, in 3 minutes or less I will tell them my story and inform them of what's to come in the next 3 videos.

Video 2: How It Works.

In this video, in 5 minutes or less I will explain the product or service that I have to offer and the benefits it provides.

Video 3: How You Earn/Testimonials.

In this video, in 3 minutes or less I will reveal to them what they could earn if they sold my products or joined my opportunity as well. Keep the compensation plan simple, do not confuse your customer. If you are not offering a business opportunity and are just selling a product or service, I would use this video to add value by providing them with a case study, or testimonial of a satisfied customer.

Video 4: Special Bonuses.

In this video, in 3 minutes or less I will list all of the bonuses they get by purchasing from me. Maybe it's a free piece of software, a bonus training video, or coaching call. This is a great video to leave your contact information on so they can easily get ahold of you. This is your chance to provide them with even more value, which will separate you from everyone else.

If you can create these videos in such a way that they can be re-purposed, and potentially used by others in need of the specific information you provide, then that is most often an even better thing to do.

Why is this process so important and necessary for you to have success if you are generating leads online?

This process is what I call, The Upfront Indoctrination, or, Credibility Building Process. It is needed so that you can turn your cold prospects into raving fans who will continue to buy your products over and over again.

When you call your leads up after this or if they see you at a live event, many of them will act surprised, excited, and like they already know you! If this does not happen, then you know your indoctrination or credibility process was not done correctly.

Back to the drawing boards you go! You will need to go back and watch the videos over again and ask yourself, "If I were my customer, would I be excited to meet me?" If the answer is no, do it over again and again until you get it right! 10 miles in the snow, remember?

This is the secret to success. You build up a tribe of customers who are anxiously waiting for what you are going to do next. And it all starts with putting your leads into this beautiful and oh so sexy process!

Just knowing what we've discussed thus far, if you execute upon it you'll be so far ahead of your competitors it's ridiculous to even think about it. I hope I have your wheels spinning a bit!

Freshmen year of Internet Marketing 101 is over! Get ready, because we are just getting warmed up.

CHAPTER 4

SOPHOMORE YEAR – MY EARLY MENTORS AND THE SWITCH THAT SPARKED MY FIRST BUSINESS IDEA

I have a few questions for you. How many mentors do you currently have? How many high-end coaches have you hired in the past two years? When I say high-end, I mean $10,000 or more invested.

Think about this: If you have not invested in a mentor, you are choosing to walk 10 miles in the snow for no reason. Do you like trenching through the snow, in the pitch dark, freezing cold, with no map? No? Then know that every great entrepreneur has a great mentor behind them. There is no reason to try to weather the storm alone.

I have a few other questions for you. Do you want people to pay *you* for mentorship? Would you like it if people were paying *you* for high-end products or coaching? Would it feel good to see $10,000 and up regularly being wired into your bank account?

One of my mentors once told me, "If you are not willing to invest in yourself, what makes you think someone else is going to invest in you?" Sage advice. I *could not* sell high-end coaching unless I was investing in it myself! Once you make the investment yourself, your confidence will skyrocket. You'll see the value you've personally received and will have no problem making a similar offer yourself, because you're simply recommending something you yourself have done and received great transformational value from. It's just like any other service. You wouldn't recommend a restaurant to a close friend unless you had been there yourself, would you?

When I'm looking for a coach or mentor, I love to send them a message that simply says, "How much?" They typically message me back, "How much for what?" My reply then is usually, "One day of your time!"

I like one-day coaching sessions the best. I get their full attention for a few hours and then I can do what I do best, which is relentlessly implement and take action.

Being committed to relentless and consistent daily action towards your goals is vastly more powerful than any other skill, tip, or tactic you will ever learn.

As you start to see some positive results in your online marketing business, the mistake I see most people making is that they stop learning with the intent of achieving mastery.

It's one thing to learn something. Yet it's an entirely different thing to learn with the intent of mastery.

You may be wondering, "What's the difference?"

Being that I'm a former athlete, comparing things to sports seems to always explain things the best.

Let's say you are a football fan, and you understand how the game is played. If that's the case, you can easily identify a run play from a pass play.

But former football players like myself are looking at the game through a different lens. When I am watching a football game, I'm viewing it through a lens of mastery. For example, I can quickly identify if a team is in a two-deep zone with man-to-man coverage underneath.

Casual fans just see a bunch of defensive players running around trying to tackle the guy on offense with the ball. And if you're a complete newbie to the sport, you just see a bunch of guys running around on a field wearing Spandex.

I've committed to putting in my 10,000 hours in this sport. Mastery. So I can quickly identify if a cornerback and the weak-side safety is cheating on the back-side of a play, and know that later on in the game the team on offense should run a play-action fake with a streak on the back-side, to take advantage of the coverage and the cheating defensive players.

And unless you understand football, you probably have no idea what I just said!

This is an example of understanding something on the surface versus understanding it with the intent of mastery. Mastery is the advantage that millionaires and billionaires have over you. It's the difference between being someone like Tom Brady and, "What's his name?" third string quarterback sitting over on the bench. And just because you're in the game doesn't make you worthy and competent enough to be at the top of the pack. Committing to mastery? That will get you there.

Now I'm no billionaire. However, I'm smart enough to know that I must continue to learn from people who are successful, and from people who learn and *fail* with the intent of mastery.

Yes, I just said you must learn from people who *fail*.

Failure is life's biggest learning lesson. This is why my favorite quote is, "The Wise Learns More From The Fool Than The Fool Learns From The Wise."

Where most people look at failure as a bad thing, I look at it as a chance to acquire wisdom of what not to do.

I have had several mentors in my life, some by choice, and some by complete accident. I hope to be *your* trusted advisor and mentor when it comes to lead generation and marketing in the future!

I encourage you to have mentors in all aspects of your life. Maybe you have a spiritual mentor. You can have a health and wellness mentor. You can have a business coach and mentor. Last but not least, you should have me as your online marketing mentor, of course!

I was very lucky to find my first online marketing mentor, Jonathan Budd. In my opinion he was the GOAT (Greatest Of All Time) when it came to online marketing. Not only did he completely understand the ins and outs of marketing, he had the little intangibles that make an entrepreneur truly great. He had a relentless work ethic that was unmatched. He had the charisma to inspire you to move mountains for him. He actually practiced what he preached. Which believe it or not, is extremely rare these days. Best of all, he wanted the absolute best for all of his students.

To this day, I do my best to bring those same characteristics to the table for all of my students! Remember, success leaves tracks.

My goal whenever I hire a mentor or a coach is to make them proud. I want to be the very best student they have ever had! When they speak at an event, do a webinar or create a product, I want them sharing my success stories to their audience. Can you adopt a similar mindset? If so, it will cause you to *act* differently. It will change your life!

And here's why: I've found that if you go into each mentoring or coaching session with that attitude, it will literally force you to commit to mastery. If you are hiring top-notch coaches, you won't become their best student ever without fully mastering what they are teaching you.

One of my proudest moments is when my mentor Jonathan Budd was speaking at an event, and a friend of mine was there and sent me a screenshot of my picture on the two big screens as he was sharing my story to over 1000 people.

I always made it a goal to do the same thing to my students when I speak at events. I love to show their videos or brag about them every chance I get. I remember how it made me feel, and based on the feedback I get from my students when I do it, I know it makes them feel good too. We all like to be recognized for our efforts. And sadly, this isn't done near enough in the workplace or even on the home-front.

The Mentor Responsible For My Millions

There is one mentor who I have known for years who is responsible for me becoming a millionaire online many times over. And that's Matt Lloyd, founder of My Online Business Education (MOBE). Matt Lloyd owns one of the largest direct sales companies in the world, earning him over 100 million dollars in revenue so far.

I have never met a person more focused on the numbers than Matt Lloyd is. We both came up in the industry around the same time and I've watched him build a business that is utterly amazing. We actually met at a VIP party during an online event where we both finished in the top 10 of an affiliate contest.

We were both "deer in the headlights" and star struck as we mingled with all of the big time marketers who we would see online. Most of the people there had no idea who we were. Somehow, Matt sparked up a conversation with me, immediately telling me about a product he was creating. Who would have thought that product would turn into a 100 million dollars and growing business today?! We kept in touch on Facebook and have been great friends ever since.

This is why I tell every entrepreneur to attend events. You never know whom you will meet and what type of relationships you can build.

I have since been a speaker at several of Matt's events including one in Fiji where I took my wife and had a blast! We even teamed up for a huge affiliate competition where we were trying to win an Audi R8. Our team of underdog entrepreneurs finished second, beating out several of the industry's greatest online marketers. This was the thing that I believe really put us on the map as serious marketers.

Matt's Million Dollar Lesson

One day we were in Las Vegas and he showed me his company dashboard, which revealed all of his day to day numbers and earnings as we were getting ready to go to dinner. He said, "Look Vince, always watch your numbers." Hmm… "Interesting," I thought. And then he went on. "We are 17% up from last month right now. I always try to break my record every month, and knowing my numbers at every second is the only way I can do it."

At the time, my company was doing 5 to 6 figures a month. Yet, Matt's company was doing that almost daily. It was incredible and inspiring to me.

So we went to dinner. And after dinner we went back to get ready to hit the town! Of course, Matt checked his company numbers first! What I saw shocked me to the core. By the time we got back to the room Matt had earned another six figures. What made that incredible was the fact that we were only gone about 45 minutes!

Let's just say I made it a point to start focusing on the numbers after that. He also told me another golden nugget that I'll never forget. He told me that the secret to wealth, is the phone. He said most people never pick up the phone. And then he said this impactful sentence to me, "Hire someone to call all of your leads, and your business will explode."

So what do you think I did? Well, I hired a person to not only call all of my leads, but to call them and thank them when they bought a product as well. He gave me some advice and I acted on it! Remember that. When you hear a good tip, implement it immediately, even if you don't have everything perfectly set up just yet.

And that tip is really what led me to create my first company that I ended up selling within two years. That business earned millions. And I owe a lot of what I did to my dear friend, Matt Lloyd.

Be sure to get Matt's Book, LIMITLESS, and tell him you heard about it from his buddy, Vince Reed.

The key lesson you should take from all of this is that you must be willing to listen and quickly execute. Money loves speed. I just love being the student first and then moving into the teacher role. It's such an amazing and profitable strategy to follow.

You may be curious as to what numbers you should be paying attention to. Below are just a few things you should be monitoring daily:

Daily Marketing Expenses (Paid Ads Only)
Cost Per Lead (Clicks Divided By Opt-in Subscribers)
Daily Leads
Monthly Leads
Daily Sales On Every Product You Offer
Phone Sales Numbers

These are what you call your KPI. Or, Key Performance Indicators.

You should always compare these numbers to the prior month. Always. If you focus on the numbers, and like my good friend Matt does, try to beat your numbers by a little bit each month, you will be well on your way to a million-dollar business. You will also know when and where you can scale up your profits, fast!

My list of individuals that have aided in my success runs very deep. And I'm quite sure I will hurt some of my mentors' feelings for not mentioning them in the next section of this book. Please forgive me. I'm very grateful for you all. Yet I only have so much room here to write. As I share some of my mentors with you, I hope two things will happen. One, these are the best of the best at what they do within our industry. Check them out, and they may be your mentors too! Two, you'll notice that I have a lot of mentors. Don't ever go about trying to figure something out all by yourself. Go straight to the top. And then figure it out with the help of the best in the world at what they do. That'll get you to where you want to go much faster.

The person who has had the biggest impact on my life recently is my good friend, Russell Brunson. I have made it a serious focus to study and master sales funnels lately. I've discovered that Russell is the best in the world at creating sales funnels that work. Because I have traffic down to a science already, learning how to create sales funnels has done wonders for my business! Thanks Russell!

Then there is my blogging coach and good friend Ray Higdon, who I quoted earlier. He has helped me turn my little blog that was generating only 20 leads per day and maybe six figures a year into a blog that generates hundreds of leads a day and seven figures a year. There is not a better blogging or business coach in the world.

Then there are people like my friend Mark Hoverson, whom I seem to always call during times of crisis! Seriously, Mark's middle name should be called Wisdom.

Then there are others that I learn from on a daily basis from afar. People like John Lee Dumas, host of Entrepreneur On Fire, who has been a three-time speaker at my events. He is responsible for not only helping me personally, but for also helping millions of others to launch their podcasts. Be sure to check out John's and my Podcasts on iTunes.

Nick Unsworth, founder of Life On Fire has truly inspired me! I actually wrote my business plan for Internet Traffic Factory on a hotel notepad while sitting at Nick's event.

There's Greg Gomez, founder of the Fast Start Summit, who I met at an event bar of all places. I bought him a beer because he had just won an award called "Experts of the Experts." So I wanted to pick his brain a bit afterwards. And he ended up giving me a lesson that he may or may not have been trying to. But it was powerful to me nonetheless. He asked me if I felt that I was the best at what I do. I emphatically replied back, "Yes! Of course!" He said, "Then let the world know that, bro!" That always stuck with me.

I can't stress enough to you the importance of having mentors that you can call on at will for guidance and direction!

I saved one of my mentors, Jeff Moore for last. He deserves a Special Tribute from me. I can still remember back when I was first starting out in this business. Jeff had this huge library full of every course, book, and training you could possibly imagine! Back then; I always called him "The Man With The Library Of Gold!" Today I call him my "Secret Weapon!"

He would let me come over there whenever I wanted to, and he invited me to forage through his book library, watch all the video trainings he had, and I could freely borrow any of his courses, some of them being quite expensive. He would listen to all of my crazy ideas and would encourage me as I talked about all of these ambitious goals I had! He's always been my secret weapon.

Jeff, I appreciate you being the ear I can always bounce ideas off of, and being that person that always gives me the confidence I need to take my business to the next level. And again, thanks for allowing me to raid your awesome library of goodies and thank you for all of your mentorship!

How To Get On Your Mentors' Radar
I always tell people there are two ways to get on the inside with a mentor:

1. You can buy your way in. (Coaching or Mentorship)
2. You can produce your way in. (Get Results)

Since number one speaks for itself, I will share with you how to execute number two:

Step 1. Make a list of the people you respect the most in your niche or field.

Step 2. Reach out to them and tell them that you are a fan of what they do.

Step 3. Buy their products.

Step 4. Implement what you learn, make a testimonial video about your results with their product, and then send it to them. Go as far as to share your results on your social media accounts and your email list.

Give that leader one week, and likely, they will be sharing your video on their social media accounts and/or personally writing you back.

If they don't get back to you, at the end of the day you will still be on their radar and will have earned their respect.

The Switch That Sparked My Early Business Idea
Now that you know some of my mentors, I want to share with you how I started to put everything I was learning into action.

As I mentioned earlier, my first online business was a business opportunity. I built that business using a four-part funnel that many of my students have used as well to indoctrinate their leads and make sales. In fact, one of my students used it to create a seven-figure business!

It's the process I revealed to you earlier in making four videos to introduce yourself to your leads. See Page 37.

1. About Me
2. How It Works
3. Compensation/Testimonial
4. Special Bonuses

I also mentioned earlier that I created a website that the network marketing company I was in had endorsed as the official training website for their entire company. This meant that every new customer was instructed to watch *my* marketing training videos as they entered the company.

The company also brought me in to do the training webinars for the entire company, with the aim to help the sales reps sell more products by leveraging the internet. As an insider, I started to become privy to things that most distributors did not know anything about.

For example, promises would be made to distributors as to when things would happen, even though there were no plans to implement things that the company was saying they were going to do.

Obviously, I did not like how the company was misleading the distributors, which ultimately led me to plan my exit strategy. I also noticed something else that sparked my next business decision. I started to see how much the company and the sales reps needed the lead generation training I was providing.

I knew then and there that I wanted to teach people outside of the company all of my lead generation methods. So many of the reps were struggling! They were being promised the world, yet sadly they had no real way to acquire new customers.

Although they were not paying me a single dime to do the training webinars for the company, I was able to build my list, and get valuable experience putting on all of these trainings to massive audiences.

I did those webinars, for free, for six months straight. And soon thereafter, it became time for me to move on and share what I was learning to the world!

I learned 2 valuable lessons during this experience:

1. I realized that I did not ever want to be tied to only one company. I vowed to always position myself to be neutral so that I could promote my products and other products as well. I would make sure I would only be actually tied to companies I personally owned.
2. I learned the true power of the story about the Gold Rush. During the Gold Rush, miners came out west to mine for gold in search of fortune. Some people found gold, most did not. It was the smart few there that were selling the picks and the shovels to the gold hungry miners who made the real fortunes. I learned to sell the picks and shovels to the miners instead of being the one mining for gold. My pick and shovel was teaching internet marketing lead generation strategies to entrepreneurs. What might yours possibly be?

So I took my list of over 25,000 people, and I launched my first lead generation training company. I was off to the races! And that was the starting point of my information-marketing career! And I haven't turned back since.

CHAPTER 5

JUNIOR YEAR – WANTING RECOGNITION BEFORE IT'S DESERVED AND MY FIRST $100,000 MONTH

Along with success comes great responsibility. This imparts the importance to keep things in perspective and always remain humble as you're building your empire. No matter how much money you're making or what you may accomplish, it should never be about *you*. It should always be about *your customer.*

You must always remember that the amount of income that you earn will be in direct proportion to the amount of value that you provide to the world. Wanna 10x your current income? Then start providing 10x value.

One of the biggest compliments that I get from many of my peers is that they say I'm very humble, considering all of my accomplishments in life thus far.

Recently I was at an event, and a guy who knew me from the internet came over to speak to me. He had a friend with him and he kept saying, "I can't believe I'm talking to Vince Reed!" And his friend asked me what it was I did.

I replied, "I'm an internet marketer; are you enjoying the event?"

Then the guy who knew me exclaimed, "Man, don't let this guy down play what he does!" Now the friend was intrigued! And he said, "Tell me more man, what do you do?!"

So I replied, "I'm an internet marketer who helps entrepreneurs generate his or her own leads online." Then the guy who knew me said, "Dude! He's downplaying it again! This guy is the King of Internet Marketing." He said, "I look at this guy like he's the Kanye West of the Internet."

If you don't know who Kanye West is, many consider him to be an icon of Rap Music. And he is known for being a little arrogant and overly confident. Cocky as they come really.

I laughed and said, "Well I don't know about the Kanye comparison, but thank you!"

Then he said, "I don't mean Kanye in terms of you being cocky or anything. I just view you as the best."

He said, "I didn't expect you to be this cool; can I get a picture with you?" I said, "Sure!"

These are the moments that let me know my commitment to mastery is paying off!

Your Time Will Come - Be Patient
When I launched my first marketing system after I had stopped doing the training for the network marketing company I was in, I made a million and one mistakes.

The launch itself was going quite amazingly, it had brought in hundreds of new clients! Sometimes people say that if they could do it all over again, they would do things differently. Because you just can't go back in time, the best thing to do then is to take everything as a learning lesson. And getting a lesson in life is as good as it gets! There is no better teacher.

My 1st marketing system that I created was set up with what is called a "Freemium Model." This means that people could join for FREE and then they could later upgrade to a premium membership if they chose to do so. I believe it was $27 a month when we first launched.

The company quickly grew to over 10,000 members! Most of them were FREE members though, and they were there for all of the FREE training I was giving them.

I remember doing the math before I launched the company. And I was thinking that if I got 30 free members a day, and three of them upgraded to premium memberships, that's 3 x $27 = $2,430 per month.

"If I can do that for 12 months straight, I will be rich!" I excitedly said to myself. I laugh at myself now as I write this, thinking about how clueless I was to business in general back then. Let me explain further.

First off, you should never make projections like this without supporting data. At the time, I had no clue about creating sales funnels. I was skilled at lead generation, but converting leads into sales was not my thing, yet.

And I had no clue about the numbers I should be paying attention to on a daily basis.

Which explains exactly why I had such a huge discrepancy between my free members and the paying members.

There was this huge difference between my free membership level and my premium level. This was extremely frustrating to me.

One huge mistake I made was that I did not offer any other products on the back-end in order to further maximize my profits. I know I left millions of dollars on the table by never offering 1-on-1 Coaching and creating stand-alone products to the community. You can say that I had learned my lesson!

Later in this book, I will reveal to you how I create my companies today. I'll show you the way that you should structure your company and your products so as to maximize your profits too.

So, although I did have a big membership base, I was not seeing my premium membership going up as I thought it would. My plan was not working out as "projected".

One issue I had not accounted for was the turn-over rate in which people would come and go. Most people are only going to stay in your continuity program, on average for 90 days. I was naive and thought these people would keep paying me forever like I would personally do.

If there were a website or system that was offering lead generation training, I was what you would call "a lifer". I was not going anywhere, because traffic and leads is the lifeblood of your business.

I quickly realized something else that shocked me. Most people are not going to do what you teach them, especially if they haven't invested enough to ensure that they will pay attention! I believe people *pay*, to pay attention. And the proof was in the pudding. Think about it. "Pay" attention. If you don't invest to play, you simply won't play in the game of money.

Although this company grew to over 25,000 free members, more than half of them rarely watched more than 30 minutes of training in their back office. I would check my video analytics and would be blown away by these statistics! Considering I would watch everything I could get my hands on if it was going to help me build my business!

Because they didn't pay for it, they didn't truly value it, and so they didn't pay attention to it. I vowed to never make this mistake again on any businesses that I would later create.

Although I may have done a lot of things wrong for this being my first go around, I believe that company was, despite me, still a success.

Your Time Will Come - Keep Grinding

After launching my first company for a split second I remember feeling a sense of entitlement. I was quickly beginning to be recognized for being a lead generation expert. Yet, I was never asked to speak at events. And I was beginning to become frustrated by that.

I remember that it would drive me to work that much harder to become the best! And really, that was one of the reasons that I started having *my own* events. I always say, "It's not about what happens to you, it's about how you react or respond when things do happen."

Another lesson my dad taught me was that you are not entitled to anything. Remember the "I Have Money. You Have Nothing." lesson that he taught me? Well this lesson he taught me meant that I would have to earn everything. Because I was not entitled to *a darn thing*.

I still made it a point to attend every event I could get to. I would be present and I would tune-in to every speaker. I would be there as the student. I've always remained hungry to learn. Just as hungry as I was before I'd earned my first dollar online.

Often when you go to events, the gurus there in attendance rarely actually watch the event itself. Many of them would rather be out in the hallway signing autographs or would prefer to be down at the bar taking down shots and chatting with other big-wig marketers.

Me on the other hand, even when I speak at events I always sit in the room the whole time, listening for fresh insights, getting valuable reminders on the fundamentals, and I'm taking copious notes of all of it. I love learning! It's a habit that most millionaires and billionaires share. And I know the edge that I have is that I not only out-learn my competitors, but I also out-execute them. Then I go and out-teach them as well. Each builds upon the other.

You can't out- execute or out- teach others if you are not investing in yourself and are constantly learning new things! Stay hungry. And stay humble. It'll serve you well!

My First Internet Marketing Conference
The very first event I went to was called The No Excuses Summit. It was in Las Vegas at the Venetian Hotel. Which by the way is still my hotel of choice whenever I go to Las Vegas.

Anyways, when I went to this event, I was making some money yet I was still flat broke. I was making just enough to cover expenses and to not die of starvation. Heck, I had to borrow money just to get to the event! Every leader and top earner in the industry was speaking at this event, including my mentor, Jonathan Budd!

So there was *no way* in hades that I was not going to be at this event. Walking through the doors, I noticed that the room was packed to the hilt, wall to wall filled with people. Chock full of hungry and motivated marketers, all looking for that one piece of information that could help take their business to the next level.

As I sat in the very back of the room, I would observe all of the "gurus" huddled in the back talking with each other. I would see them laughing and joking at the bar. These were all of the top earners online in one place at the same time.

I started to research them all to see what made them different from me or anyone else at the event. One thing that I quickly discovered was that each one of them had a very specialized and specific skill set.

I also noticed that the only person who was really teaching lead generation was my mentor, Jonathan Budd.

So I knew at that time what I had to do if I ever wanted to get on that stage. I had to become a total master at something! Right then and there is when I decided that lead generation was going to be my skill of choice. My forte, if you will.

After that event, I was committed to become the best ever when it came to marketing and lead generation training. My goal was to have people picture me whenever they were thinking about marketing and lead generation. Just the same way people think of Michael Jordan whenever they are asked who is the greatest basketball player of all time. He would immediately pop up in most people's minds. And that's what I wanted to happen with me.

Yes, I know this was an ambitious goal! But if you don't think or play big, you normally never get in the game at all.

I remember thinking that if I ever got asked to speak, I would want to make sure I delivered content so good that people could quickly implement it and put it into action that same day.

When I first started to attend events, I was never a fan of the personal development speeches. I already worked hard, so I didn't feel like I needed someone telling me what I was already doing. I didn't need a pep talk to help get my butt into gear. I simply wanted the how-to information that would put money in my pockets. Now I realize that personal development is just as important as the technical, how-to information. It all starts with your mindset. And if you don't have the right internal framework for success, then you will get chewed up and spit out when it comes to business and life in general.

In working with many people I've found out that many business owners simply are not cut out to be entrepreneurs. The second they get hit in the mouth with adversity, they quit or blame someone else. As an entrepreneur, the first rule you must remember is that it's always your fault. Always!

Think about it this way: If you were to build a 7-figure business from scratch, would you want the credit? If you want the credit for success, then you must take the credit and the blame for the failures also!

Now it took me several years to become a speaker at an event. And I am still humbled every time I speak, and I often even get choked up! Today, I seem to be speaking at events on a monthly basis and I continue to host my own events as well.

Many of the speakers that I saw huddled around in the back of that first event back when I was dead broke, now speak at *my* events.

And I often speak at their events as well! It feels good to give back. I never allow the event host to pay for me to attend or to pay for my room, because I'm just honored to be there contributing. One of my favorite things about events is the Taxi or Uber ride to the event; it keeps me humble and hungry!

Just to put a cherry on top of this story, let me tell you what happened next.

I eventually became a speaker at No Excuses Summit. It took me six years to be invited to speak there, but I did grace the NES stage! It was a huge honor for me because this is where it all started. It was there that I decided I was going to make internet marketing my career.

This story gets even better. After building one of my companies for two years, up to making it the #1 lead generation training company for home business professionals; it was eventually acquired by the parent company of No Excuses Summit, and we ended up doing a Co-Branded event together to celebrate the merger!

One year after speaking at No Excuses 6, No Excuses 7 and my event, Internet Traffic Live 3 combined to have one of the greatest events ever, doing something that had never been done before! Merging two events to have one explosive and value-packed weekend!

Every top speaker in the industry spoke at the event, and this was one of the proudest moments of my life.

As the No Excuses Summit lives on, I can move on knowing that I was there in the beginning and was able to play a huge part in it's long term success.

Like always, my goal is to be the #1 student to all of my mentors; but this goal goes for events too. I think I may have accomplished that goal here with NES! Hopefully I've been their #1 success story!

I'm telling you this story to ensure to you that your time will come also. Your job is to make sure that you are *prepared* to take advantage of it when the opportunity comes knocking!

My First $100,000 Month

As my business started to grow, I was beginning to have some very profitable months, all while working from the comforts of my own home. I'm talking more money in a single day than most people earn in a single month, and in some cases, a year!

I always had a goal to earn 6-figures in a single month. I know to some that sounds crazy. But once you learn how to do it, it's not as hard as you may think.

Remember, when you are selling products online your business is global and sales can come in 24/7/365. I will never forget the day early on in my business when I earned $3,000 on Christmas. That was when I knew I truly had a global business.

So how did I do it?

The first thing I had to do was identify the numbers I needed to hit in order to reach my goal of $100,000 in a single month; based on the products I had to offer at the time.

When I ask students how much money they want to make, the most popular answer that I get is $10,000 per month. I then ask them how they are going to reach that goal, and they say something like, get more leads, or talk to more people, or I need to create my own product.

The truth is, those things are important, but they are not what's going to get you to $100,000 per month!

$100,000 in one month means I must average $3,333 per day for 30 days. This can happen in numerous ways.

Below are some of the scenarios:

33 Sales At $100 Per Day

7 Sales At $500 Per Day

3 Sales At $1000 Per Day

1 Sales Of $3,333 Per Day

But more importantly, it starts with how you *frame* what it is that you have to offer.

For example, you could say you need to sell 7 items at $500 per day to make $100,000/month. Or, you could ask yourself these 2 simple questions:

1. How many people are currently buying products like what I have to offer daily?

2. Would X number of those people buying my type of products right now want my products if they knew it existed?

If the answer to question number 1 is in the millions, then you have a market that will allow you to earn $100,000 per month.

The truth is, you only need a small percentage of a large market to earn millions of dollars.

This is what I did. I focused on the numbers, and I realized that I needed more products in order to hit my income goals.

Think of it this way, if you walk into a grocery store, and the only thing in the store is bread, would you want to shop there? Even though bread is considered the most purchased item in a grocery store, most people would not want to shop there if that is all they offered. And if that is all they offered, they'd be missing out on a lot of profits as people would then go somewhere else to get everything else they needed. So in most circumstances, you will need more products than just something like bread if you want to maximize your profits. I'm not saying you need millions of products like a grocery store, but you do need more than one based on my experience.

You should not focus on 1-off product sales. You should always be trying to get 2-for-1 customers. This means if you sell bread, you should also offer lunch meat, or peanut butter and jelly with every loaf you sell. Things that complement the original item and add to its value.

Some people call this an upsell. I call it "common sense" today; but as you saw from my first business, I was not doing this from the very start. You can learn from my mistakes.

Another example: If I were selling an information product, I could offer a piece of software, or a bonus training on a different topic that is hyper-congruent with the original purchase to further assist the customer. The product may teach the customer how to do something. And the Software -one time offer- may do all of the manual labor for them. The first product may show how to run a profitable Facebook Ad. And the bonus training could be how to create a profitable Fan Page, thus nicely complementing the first offer.

So in other words, if I were selling bread, I would not offer to sell them bedroom furniture as an upsell. Because that would *not* be congruent.

By doing this, I am able to get 2-for-1 sales. Which allows the number of sales needed to reach my $100,000 per month goal to essentially be cut in half. And this would raise my revenue with every purchase, even if every customer didn't take me up on the upsell offer. And this would be offering tremendous extra value to the customer as well!

This is the same strategy McDonald's and other fast food restaurants use when they ask if you want a combo or a milkshake with your order. "Would you like to supersize that?" Is a one-time upsell offer. That simple sentence has made them Billions. What complementary and valuable offer could you have in your business?

After I closed down my first company, I launched an app company which would build personal apps for entrepreneurs to brand themselves and bring them leads.

The company launched with a different type of pay model. I offered a yearly payment of $297 for app training, and then customers could pay $497 and $47 per month for their app and hosting.

We barely made any sales in the first week. So I thought it was going to be a complete flop. I was honestly worried about the business and was having nightmares of it failing before it even got started. I then made a tweak to the entry-level price point, that to be honest, was better for the company. And then, what happened? The company took off like a rocket!

This let me know a lot about how people view value and how they see numbers!

Here's how I did it. I lowered the entry-level training to a $19 trial for 30 days; and then it would go to $97 per month. When the original price was just $297 per year for the training, barely anyone took the offer. The new deal was lower upfront, but $1,164 per year before they even purchased an app.

Then there was a time sensitive discount on the app for $497, and $47 per month for hosting. This price I made available for 7 days. And then the price of the app would go to $797 if they didn't purchase it within the first 7 days.

After making less than $10,000 in the first week, we then went on to earn close to $146,000 in the last three weeks.

Thus allowing me to hit my goal of $100,000 per month! I tell you this story to let you know that sometimes, what *you* see as valuable, your customers may see the exact opposite.

The lesson in this story is to know your numbers! And don't be afraid to make changes that others may not see the value in!

CHAPTER 6

SENIOR YEAR – 7 FIGURES IN 1 YEAR AND HOSTING MY FIRST EVENT

Although my app company went on to generate over 7-figures, I don't really consider it a true 7-figure business, and here's why:

Quite a few of the top earners and gurus promoted that company, and my success was largely based on a huge push from these super affiliates. Being that I'm a competitive and honest guy, I do not rightly feel that I can take credit for that company's success.

I can take *some* of the credit of course, but not all of it!

A lot of top earners who do multiple 7-figure product launches do not credit their affiliates for their success. If you were to take those affiliates away, they would have a hard time even remotely hitting close to those 7-figure numbers. I understand that, and I always thought about that as my app company started to take off.

Would this company be successful *without* a huge affiliate push? Would this be a sustainable business for me?

My honest assessment now is, yes. But back then my answer would have been, no.

I eventually closed my app company because I saw several red flags that I did not prepare for when I got started. In fact, I pulled the plug while it was still generating 6-figures per month. People around me thought I was crazy to literally cancel over $50,000 in residual income payments.

For me, it's never been all about the money. It's always been about providing value to the customer and not putting them in a place where the walls could come crashing down on them later down the road.

The Red Flags

Looking back, the app company was a great idea and an amazing concept. That is why so many partners and affiliates got behind it. A personal app for individual business owners where you could stream live videos or do push notifications to all of your customers' phones!

This concept was the first of its kind.

Why did I close the company then?

Everything was great until Apple and Android started to change the rules. iTunes stopped accepting and approving personal apps in their app store. This meant that we had a huge problem, which caused us to change course right away.

We found that we had to make HTML5 versions of the app for iTunes users. This created additional hurdles that we had to overcome to allow those apps to have the same features as the Android users had.

Android was fine with approving the apps, but if you are going to have an app company, you have to get *all* of your apps approved.

What made matters worse is that some apps would get approved in iTunes and others would not. And the problem was they would not tell us why this was happening. All I could think about was another Real Estate crisis. But this time, it would be me selling thousands of apps only to have them get denied in the iTunes marketplace afterwards!

This was only one of many fires that I had with this company. Another potential problem was that we were outsourcing the development of the apps, which pushed our company revenue margins down to under 20%, depending on the app.

This was not anyone's fault other than my own. I negotiated the deal, and to be frank, I did a horrible job at it. I knew I was not going to be the one developing the apps, so I needed a distributor I could trust. Today, I'm a much better negotiator because of it, and I would never had made that deal if it were to have been presented to me again. In reality, they would have done the deal for a lot less than what I paid them for. They made a lot of money in a very short period of time!

Here's a quick tip on negotiating. Never show your hand first! It's just like playing Poker. Let them offer what they would do the job for, and always make a lower counter offer no matter what. But you must be willing to walk away from the negotiating table. You can't seem needy or desperate.

In this case, I showed my hand first. And they jumped all over it.

I learned that it's best to keep your company margins around 50%. Some people may say that's too high. Yet, if you structure your company this way, you will never have cash flow issues.

I'm telling you this because some of you have goals of earning millions of dollars. But sometimes making millions is not all what it is cracked up to be! I learned very quickly that it's not about how much money you make, it's about how much you keep.

I also realized how important it was to not be reliant on just one "invaluable resource." You never want to be dependent on other people to keep your business afloat. I'm not saying not to trust others. But what I am saying is if you build a company that is dependent on one person, and they quit, it is your fault as the company owner if the business crumbles to the ground and disintegrates into dust.

So yes, I closed down a million-dollar business before it became a 10-million-dollar disaster full of unhappy customers and affiliates.

You've got to know when to hold 'em and know when to fold 'em! The good news is, I learned *a lot* of lessons from that experience. Knowledge, acquired!

Hire Slow But Fire Fast

I will be the first to tell you that I have not always followed this rule. But this book is about you learning from my mistakes. And as you have read, I have made a ton of them.

I have hired a lot of great people and I have also hired some complete losers. Guys that should have a giant "**L**" on their foreheads to inform people of their character.

Because of my extreme loyalty I used to keep people around way too long. There are a few rules I've developed in my company on hiring. Remember them, and you may not make the same costly mistakes that I made!

Rule number 1 is to avoid at all costs hiring family or friends. Seriously, don't do it. I don't care who you are, it's not easy to fire aunt Betty or cousin Bob. Or wife Sue.

Family BBQs and get-togethers will never be the same, as you are now to blame for a family member losing their home and being broke! And you ate the last of the BBQ to top it off.

So, how do you hire the right people? Well thankfully, there is a lot of talent outside of your family gene pool.

I love to hire interns for FREE and train them. Give them a small task and see how they handle it. Then slowly introduce more tasks to them.

My right and left hand man Vinny Aiello started out working with me as an intern when he was still in college. He started working with me after I let go of a close family friend who was working with me, and who seemed to have a "hard time" being punctual.

People who know me understand that the fastest way to take me from 0 to 100 is to not be punctual.

So when I brought him in as an intern I told him 3 things:

1. I'm not going to be easy on you.
2. I want you to be a problem solver.
3. Don't ever be late, period.

There was one more thing I told him…

I told him that he would not be getting paid. "I will teach you how to be a millionaire. And that's worth more than a paycheck." I said.

He said yes to every demand. And not only did he work for free, but he worked for free for two summers straight, in between training for his upcoming football seasons.

When he graduated college, he came into my office expecting me to give him a paying job to get started, and I told him, "No."

He asked me, "Why?"

I told him, "You need real world, 9 to 5 experience Vinny!" Then I said, "Come back in one year and we can chat then." As much as I wanted to hire him right then and there on the spot, I didn't. Although I'm sure he was not happy about it, he thanked me for the experience, and he landed a good job with all of the shiny benefits and solid salary within just a few short weeks.

Fast forward a year later and he called me up and wanted to come talk to me about an app idea he had. This was when I was on the verge of closing the app company mind you. As he was telling me about his app idea, to be honest, I was not listening as closely as I should have been.

I was too busy thinking about how I was going to break it to him that I wanted him to come back and work with me. I could tell that he was ready!

I could clearly see that although he was working in a 9 to 5 with all the benefits of being safe and secure, he was in my office asking me about an entrepreneurial venture that he was interested in. "Aha! Yes, my boy!"

This is what I was looking for in a potential partner. I always viewed Vinny as more than an intern. From day one, I could see that he was potentially the person who I could train to run my entire company after I'm long gone.

Once he was done telling me about his idea, I simply said, "Your idea sounds interesting, but I have a better question for you. Are you ready to come work with me now?"

I seriously don't think I would have made that offer if he were still in love with his corporate job.

He said, "YES!" And he was working full-time with me two weeks later.

He came to work with me even though I cut his pay by a third, and I was not offering a full benefits package either.

His starting base pay? $2,500 per month.

Within a few months he was earning 4 times that. And now he drives a Mercedes and nothing goes down unless he and I say so. Vinny is now a boss baby and a huge part of Internet Traffic Factory and quite frankly anything else I do from now on in life and business. He's earned my trust!

Everything that kid has received from me, he has earned. He reminds me of me when I got started! I love that kid like a son.

Thanks Vinny for all you have done and continue to do!

My First Live Event

Once Vinny started working with me, things started to move a lot faster in my company. Before he came aboard I would out-source a lot of my busy work. I would shoot and edit my own videos. And I'd personally handle a ton of other little things that would come up every day.

I was literally a One-Man Show!

Now with Vinny there, I had help. And this allowed me to focus more on revenue generating activities.

As I closed down my app company Vinny and I started to work on a new business that I'd wanted to create. I wanted to take all of the things I had done wrong in past businesses and eliminate them from this new venture! And then I'd incorporate all the good things I had learned along the way.

I was going to make sure that I was not dependent on anyone else this time! I also would make sure that I had the right type of products to offer which would keep the company profitable, long term.

My original plan was to start training Real Estate Agents on how to get listings using the Internet.

Being that I had a Real Estate background and based on my early research, there were no internet marketers teaching internet marketing strategies focused on getting listings or on how to sell Real Estate online.

Most were still using old school methods, and the extent of their internet marketing efforts was to list a property on the MLS and then do an open house!

Vinny and I spent months slaving away to create this company. And just one day before we planned to launch? I changed my mind. Vinny got to the office on time as he always did, and I told him the news that we were not going to launch that Real Estate training company. He asked me, "Why not, Vince?" I told him that I wanted to keep training people in the Home Business space! "I feel I have more that I want to give them," I said. "I don't like what's being taught, and I can't leave them just yet!" I continued on telling him.

Like always, he said "Okay. Let's get to work." He never questioned me or showed any resistance. So that day in my office on my big whiteboard, we created My Internet Traffic System, which was the company that I ended up selling two years later.

That company earned millions and we've helped thousands of people all over the world!

We launched My Internet Traffic System on January 1, and we booked our first live event for April 23, only three months from our start date!

I had never hosted my own live event before. And to be honest, the thought of having one freaked me out. My friend Matt Lloyd would always tell me to do my own live events.

I can hear Matt's Australian accent right now saying, "Just do it, Vince. Do an event. You can do it mate!"

So I met with an event coordinator, and I signed the contract for my first ever event. So now I was on the hook to do this thing! I had no where to go but forward. And there is a big lesson in that. Commit yourself to something in a way where there's no other option but to do it! It's a little trick of the ultra-successful.

So we started to do a little marketing and quickly sold 50 tickets, which was the size I was shooting for. Yet, the event ended up having over 75 people attend which surprised even me considering I barely even promoted it!

When I got to the hotel the day before the event was supposed to start, I remember being afraid to go downstairs to the reception area out of fear that no one was going to show up.

Can you imagine the fear of getting ready to go on stage and nobody is out in the audience? Or worse, just one or two people are there waiting for you, the supposed Guru? Yeah. That fear was following me around all over the place.

As I walked down there, I didn't see anyone. And then, all at once, groups of people started coming out from around the corner. And all of my nerves instantly melted away.

The following year, we had over 200 people. And in our third year we had 450 people. Since then I've gone on to have private masterminds as well! Events are no longer a struggle for me, but it didn't become easy until I took action and did one!

Now I can breathe.

As you read this, I want you to know that *anything* is possible. I am living proof of that.

CHAPTER 7

THE PRESENT - GRADUATE SCHOOL YEAR 1:
THERE HAS TO BE A BETTER WAY - THE INCOME
MAXIMIZER FORMULA

W hat you have read so far are true events that have taken place in my past. Now I want to move you into the present.

As we start to dig a lot deeper into the how-to training, I want you to understand that all of my business accomplishments took place over a 8-year time frame. I started my online business full time in 2008 and as I sit here writing this it's 2016

There are no overnight success stories, although it can appear that way sometimes. Don't ever doubt your efforts, you are where you are supposed to be. And all you can do is focus on your next move. My goal is that this book shortens your learning curve, drastically.

At this point in my life, I have created multiple 7-figure businesses, I've hosted my own live events, and now I have written my first book.

Making money online for me at this point in my life as crazy as it may sound is easy. With that being said, I don't expect it to be easy for most people. Most people could not match the time I have put into my business.

I had a friend ask me if I did drugs, because he had never seen a person work like me. He thought I might be like Bradley Cooper's character in the movie, Limitless. I am typically up at 5am and I'm up most nights working deep into the night. I love what I do because I know that it works and that it can change people's lives!

With that being said, my job as your trusted advisor when it comes to marketing and lead generation is to give you information that will make your road to success much smoother than mine was.

One day I woke up and I decided to look back at my business and try to figure out a formula to help people build their own 7-figure business.

Being that I had built million dollar companies multiple times, I knew what to do and how to do it for myself. But I didn't have a way to articulate how or what I was doing so that anyone could simply mirror my efforts and get similar results.

So I started writing down some of the things I did, some of the characteristics a person needed, and things that I deemed necessary for anyone to create a 7-figure business.

After pages and pages of notes, I came up with the conclusion that it would take a complete newbie at least 3 years to build a 7-figure business if they followed my formula.

I called this formula my Income Maximizer Formula. It will reveal the exact steps a person must follow to build a 7-figure business in 3 years or less!

The cool thing about this formula is that I've had numerous top earners and complete newbies do the formula, and every time it's been spot on.

So I have a question for you right now:

If I could show you how to build a 7-figure business using the Internet in 3 years or less, would that interest you?

If your answer is yes, you're in luck. Because I'm about to reveal to you exactly how the formula works.

The Back Story Of The Income Maximizer Formula

When I graduated from college and moved to Los Angeles with my brother, he gave me a book called Rich Dad Poor Dad, written by Robert Kiyosaki. It was the book that sparked my interest in becoming an entrepreneur.

I read that book in just two days, which was the fastest I had ever read an entire book before! In the book, he mentioned another book he had written called, Cashflow Quadrant. It focused on the secrets to acquiring wealth.

There were two sides and four parts to the Quadrant.

The left side consisted of the employee and the self-employed individuals. These were people who traded their time for dollars. Unfortunately, this way of thinking and living is the way most people are programmed for from birth. The whole idea of going to school so you can get a good job approach, which keeps most of society stuck in the rat race.

The right side consisted of the business owners and investors. These were people who allowed money to work for them. They pay for things with assets, and they don't rack up huge liabilities.

Never, in my opinion was there a book that broke down the steps to financial freedom in such a simple way.

I loved the book, but I felt that the concepts were too broad. I believe that a motivated entrepreneur could take the book, read between the lines, and go out into the world and fail their way to success, as I did. I took the ideas from that book and I ran with it! And I made it a point to get to the *right* side of the quadrant. But I can see how others could read it, enjoy the "concepts", but still be confused as to where to actually start.

What I've found in my several years of running a business is that people need to be told the exact steps they need to take. That is why I came up with the Income Maximizer Formula. Here's how it works…

The formula has 5 parts or sections:

1: Influence & Network
2: Skill Level
3: Consistency
4: List Size
5: Marketing Spend

Each section is scored on a 1 to 10 point system. Depending on what your score is within the 10-point system, you are allotted points from 1 to 3. So for example, if I were to ask you to grade yourself from 1 to 10 on how you view your Influence & Network in your industry or niche market, with 10 being the highest, what would it be?

See the point system below:

1 -3 = 1 Point
4 – 7 = 2 Points
8 – 10 = 3 Points

Let's say you give yourself an 8. This would be based on your own perception of where you believe you are. As I provide you with details about the Income Maximizer Formula, it will tell you exactly where you are. And it's often a lot lower than where people will grade themselves upon first thought!

In this case, if you were to grade yourself as an 8 before knowing the criteria of each point system, you would get 3 points for the Influence and Network category.

If you had graded yourself as a 4 out of 10, you would be allotted 2 points for that category.

The formula will breakdown each one of the categories so you will not have to guess on your score in each section. You will know exactly what you need to do and how long you will need to be doing it. This way you never have to guess when it comes to you scoring yourself on the 10-point system.

Each part is scored individually, and once each section is complete you must add up your score. This score will reveal to you what your current income level is, and what you need to do to get to the next income bracket.

The highest score you can get is 15 points. That would mean you would have scored a 3 in each section, as there are 5 sections.

The Income Chart Is Below:

14 - 15 Points: 7 Figures
11 - 13 Points: 6 Figures
7- 10 Points: 5 Figures
1 - 6 Points: 5 Figures

So, after completing the formula and figuring out your score, if your score were an 8 after adding up all your points in each section, you would likely be earning a 5-figure income. It could be $99,000 a year, or $11,000.

So let's eliminate the guesswork and break down this formula! By the end of this chapter you will know exactly what you need to do to become a millionaire within 3 years or less. I hope this excites you and lights a fire under you to get started right away!

Network & Influence

It's no secret that you are who you associate with. I noticed a *huge* increase in my income when I upped my network. When I started attending events, hiring coaches, and attending high-end masterminds, my income and my network drastically changed for the better!

The scoring criteria for Network & Influence:

1: Are You Invited To Speak At Or Do You Host Your Own Live Events

Are people calling you and inviting you to speak at their events or are you hosting your own events?

2: Do You Have A Huge Authority Rolodex

If I were to call you and ask you for guidance, do you have authority figures on speed dial ready to take your call?

3: Currently A 7-Figure Earner

I'm yet to meet a 7-figure earner who does not have major influence in their niche. Have your earned a minimum of 7-figures in a single year?

4: Easily Get 200 People On A Call Or Webinar

If you can send an email or do a status update and get 200 people on a call or webinar, you are an influencer and your network is on point. Can you do this?

How You Grade Yourself: Out of the 4 criteria above, how many of these traits do you possess?

When grading yourself on a 1 to 10 point system:

1 -3 = 1 Point
4 – 7 = 2 Points
8 – 10 = 3 Points

How to accurately grade yourself: See how many of the 4 questions above meet your specific situation.

3 Out Of 4 = 3 Points
2 Out Of 4 = 2 Points
1 Out Of 4 = 1 Point

If I were to ask you where you graded yourself before you knew the criteria, and you were to give yourself an 8 out of 10, that means you would have to have met 3 out of the 4 criteria in this section.

I encourage you to be honest with your assessment!

Be sure to go back now and figure out your score. You can write down your score here:

_____

Skill Level
As I mentioned earlier, it's important for you to master a specific skill. When a person meets you, they should know exactly how you can help them better than anyone else can.

When people think of me, I want them to immediately think of me as the best in the world at helping entrepreneurs get targeted traffic and leads for their businesses.

If a client were to ask you what it is that you do that makes you the best in the world, what would your reply to them be?

The scoring criteria for Skill Level:

Skill Level is based on 3 categories with another criteria being based on time invested. In my opinion, it takes 3 years to become a master at anything. So unless you meet all 3 of the criteria below and you have been doing it for 3 years, you cannot give yourself 3 points. If you meet all 3 criteria and have only been perfecting your skill for 2 years, you will get a 2. If you meet all 3 criteria but have only been doing it for 1 year, then you will automatically get a 1 for this section.

So in other words, if you just started perfecting your skill this year, you are getting 1 point for this section.

Time Invested: 1 Year, 2 Years, Or 3 Years

Experience *does* matter. There is no such thing as an overnight success story in business. You have to be willing to put in the wrench time.

1: Invested A Minimum Of $10,000 In Your Education

Do you have mentors that you have hired or courses that you have bought that totals $10,000 or more?

2: A Specialized Skill

If I were to call you for help, what specifically could you help me with? You must identify the exact reasons people would want to work with you.

3: 10 Or More Success Stories

Could I call a minimum of 10 people who have used what you teach and achieved a positive result? Are there 10 or more videos out there of people leaving you or your company testimonials?

How You Grade Yourself: Out of the 3 criteria above, how many of these traits do you now possess?

When grading yourself on a 1 to 10 point system

1 -3 = 1 Point
4 – 7 = 2 Points
8 – 10 = 3 Points

How to accurately grade yourself

3 Out Of 3 = 3 Points
2 Out Of 3 = 2 Points
1 Out Of 3 = 1 Point

Do not forget to calculate "Time Invested" into your score for this section.

Be sure to go back now and figure out your score. You can write down your score here

———

Consistency

Consistency will play a huge part in your overall success. This is why it's very important to change your habits if you want to become a millionaire. If you do what broke people do, guess what? You will be broke. And the #1 trait of broke people is that they have bad habits and are not consistent!

Results can only come from meaningful actions being made. And the more consistent you are with those actions; the more money you will make.

The scoring criteria for Consistency:

Consistency is also based on 3 categories with another criteria being based on time invested. It takes 3 years of you being consistent to really put a dent in your marketplace. So unless you meet all 3 of the criteria below and you have been doing it for 3 years, you cannot give yourself 3 points. If you meet all 3 criteria and have only been consistent for 2 years, you will get a 2. If you meet all 3 criteria but have only been consistent for 1 year, you automatically get a 1 for this section.

1: Consistent Webinars Or Company Events

Are you consistently putting on webinars or showcasing your products and services on a weekly or monthly basis? I have done a weekly webinar for my customers every week for over 5 years.

2: Consistent Value Based Content

Are you releasing a newsletter or blog posts about your products or services on a daily, weekly, or monthly basis?

There has not been a week in the last 5 years that I have not released either a blog post or some other type of value based content. What is value based content? It is some sort of valuable information that you will be teaching your audience based what you have learned or is based on something new happening within your business.

3: Daily Or Weekly List Broadcasts

Are you consistently staying in contact with your list of customers or subscribers on a daily or monthly basis? If you are not messaging them, know that someone else is!

How You Grade Yourself: Out of the 3 criteria above, how many of these traits do you possess?

When grading yourself on a 1 to 10 point system

1 -3 = 1 Point
4 – 7 = 2 Points
8 – 10 = 3 Points

How to accurately grade yourself

3 Out Of 3 = 3 Points
2 Out Of 3 = 2 Points
1 Out Of 3 = 1 Point

Be sure to go back now and figure out your score. You can write down your score here

———

List Size

List size is simple. How many email subscribers do you have? If you were to push a button and send out an email, how many inboxes would you reach? If you are not actively building a list, yet are investing money in advertising, then you are throwing a lot of money down the toilet. Flush, down it goes...

The money and the power is in your list. Yet the true fortune is in the follow-up! I will dive further into this later on in the book.

The scoring criteria for List Size:

The best thing about list size is that this category is based on things that you can fully control!

1: 25,000 + Leads = 3 Points

If you have more than 25,000 subscribers, you would give yourself 3 Points

2: 5,000 To 25,000 Leads = 2 Points

If you have between 5,000 and 25,000 subscribers, you would give yourself 2 Points

3: 1 To 5,000 Leads = 1 Point

If you have between 1 and 5,000 subscribers, you would give yourself 1 Point

Grade yourself based on how many leads you have. Score yourself accordingly to the scale above.

Be sure to go back now and figure out your score. You can write down your score here

_____

Marketing Spend

This section is also very simple. How much money are you investing into your marketing every month? I've noticed over the years that unsuccessful companies try to figure out how to spend as little as they possibly can on marketing because they view it as an expense. The truth is, your goal as a company is to figure out how to spend as much as you can! More, not less.

The scoring criteria for Marketing Spend:

Marketing Spend is another category that is based on things that you can fully control!

1: $10,000 Per Month + = 3 Points

I've never met a successful sustainable 7-figure business that was not spending a minimum of 5 figures per month on marketing. Period.

2: $2,500 To $10,000 Per Month = 2 Points

If you are stuck in the 6-figure range with your business, I can nearly predict that this is the range where your marketing spend is for your business.

3: $0 - $2,500 = 1 Point

This is perfect when getting started, but it does not pack a big enough punch to really bring you solid product and brand recognition.

Be sure to go back now and figure out your score. You can write down your score here

_____

Grade yourself based on how much you are investing into your business, and score yourself accordingly to the scale above.

Now I want you to go back and tally up your score! See where you need to make improvements on. Maybe it's the fact that you just need more time. Possibly you need to be spending more money in your marketing efforts. You could need to focus more on actively building up your list. Find out whatever it is for you.

1 or 2 points could be the difference between 5 to 6 figures, or even 6 to 7 figures!

After reading this, your perspective on where you are in your business may have changed drastically.

Maybe you realize that you are just a few tweaks away from becoming a millionaire! Maybe you are a little freaked out because you realized you are much farther away from your goals than you thought.

With that being said, I want you to realize that there are several different ways to reach your goals. What I just shared with you has proved to be accurate for many entrepreneurs, including myself. But that does not mean it has to take you 3 years to become a millionaire!

It certainly does not take me that long to build 7-figure businesses anymore. That's because I have built a lot of these different criteria up to the point where I get things done a lot faster these days.

What you will notice is that as you get started, things may be tough. As you continue to gain experience though, as long as you don't cut corners things will get a *lot* easier.

The Income Maximizer Formula will put you in a great place to start off from! It will help you to see where you currently are in your journey to millions. And there is no better place to start from than accepting where you are truly at. The present reality, as is. Not where you "believe" yourself to be. Clarity equals true power. And now armed with clarity and seeing where you can go from here, you can now start the formula.

If you got value from the Income Maximizer Formula, be sure to message me your score by sending me a direct message on Facebook to my Fan Page!

Facebook.com/VinceReedLive

CHAPTER 8

GRADUATE SCHOOL YEAR 2 – PROVE IT VINCE - AND
THE SECRET TO STANDING OUT

One of the best things you can do as an entrepreneur is to come to grips with who you are as a person, and who you are as a business owner.

Are you a ruthless, cutthroat type of leader and person? Are you the nice and understanding type? Do you like to shine in the spotlight? Or are you the puppet master, the mastermind pulling all of the strings from behind the scenes?

The faster you identify who you are, the quicker you can embrace your strengths and can let your employees and the people around you know. Otherwise, your employees and other people who work with you may see you the complete opposite of the way you see yourself, and they won't trust you. Not one iota!

If your employees and customers don't know, like, and trust you, they won't work for you for long, and they won't buy your products.

A big part of understanding who you are means that you identify how you will deal with situations, especially when things are not going so well.

It's easy to be a certain way when things are going great for you. The question is, do you flip the script when things are *not* going your way?

For example, in my opinion, Donald Trump is a pretty ruthless entrepreneur. When I say ruthless, I don't mean he is a bad person. However, he is willing to get things done by any means necessary! And he has no problem hurting anyone's feelings as long as he's living his truth.

Want to know how he can get away with a cutthroat type of business perception?

It's because he makes it 100% clear how it's going to be from the very beginning. And if you cross him, he will have no problem saying "You're fired." He's just being himself!

This is what makes Donald Trump stand out in the crowd. The truth is, people who are not being truthful about who they are, they try to act a certain way around others. But when things go bad, they try to become like Donald Trump, and it just won't work for them.

Donald Trump is almost always true to himself. That's how he can get so much attention and stand apart from his competition. He's being authentic!

If you have the opposite personality of a Donald Trump, you can still stand out in the crowd. I look at a guy like Mark Cuban, billionaire and owner of the basketball team, the Dallas Mavericks. From what I've read and seen about Mark Cuban, he's just as tough as Donald Trump is. Yet, he chooses to take a different approach to dealing with people than Donald Trump does.

I believe the thing that makes Mark stand out is that he is able to relate to his audience by allowing himself to be vulnerable. He can be in a t-shirt at a Dallas Mavericks game screaming as if it were his very first basketball game. Then you can turn the channel and see him on Dancing With The Stars doing the foxtrot. And yet the next day, you may see him being interviewed on a local morning news show sharing an important business tip.

When you see him, you can tell that he's being his authentic self!

So the question is, how can you stand out and still remain true to your authentic self?

It all starts with you identifying who you are. And then realizing that you will not make everyone happy. That's okay! Making everyone happy is not your job. Your job is to make an impact and provide the most value to your customers as you possibly can.

How can you do this successfully?

The key is to focus on being the best at what you do. But to stand out, you must also be willing to deliver the information or product in a way that disrupts the industry norm.

In other words, what can you do that other people in your industry are not doing, and that makes your competitors a little uncomfortable?

Case in point: You won't see many entrepreneurs speak like Donald Trump. And you won't see many billionaires strutting their stuff on Dancing With The Stars.

Standing Out In A Crowd
When I made the decision that I wanted to be known as the best in the world at helping entrepreneurs generate traffic and leads, I knew I was going to have to do things that the average marketing and lead generation coaches were not willing to do. I'd have to stand out from the crowd. I'd have to be the fresh voice in a room full of nothing but dull noise.

So the first thing I did was I made a list of what I saw most of them doing. Then I wrote down on another piece of paper things that I knew they would not do.

List Of Things Other Marketing Coaches Do:

- Create Products
- Weekly Blog Posts
- Occasional Webinars
- Product Launches

- Live Interview with Leaders
- Make Result Claims

List Of Things I Knew They Wouldn't Do:

- Master All Traffic Methods
- Multiple Webinars a Week
- Daily Live Videos
- Show Their Numbers
- Show Their Results

These are just a few things that I noticed. And I knew if I did the things they were not willing to do, then I could separate myself from all of the other lead generation coaches out there.

Before I get into the specifics as to what I did to stand out, I want you to be aware of something I noticed when I started to attend high-end mastermind groups. I always try to be in the moment. I watch and listen closely to what people are saying. But more importantly, I study what they are *doing*.

I started to realize that most of the "gurus" out there teaching marketing strategies and other business strategies were not the ones actually doing the things in their business that they were teaching!

For example, the lead generation coach was not the one actually doing the marketing; and the sales training guru was not actually the one doing the sales. It was almost as if they were merely the face in front of these massive organizations. I'm not saying this is bad because I'm all for outsourcing. Yet I knew this gave me a huge advantage. It allowed me to provide value as an insider and share things that some of my competitors did not know about, because they were not doing it themselves. They weren't down in the trenches getting their hands dirty everyday like I was.

They would hire agencies to do the marketing for them, and they had phone rooms to do all of the selling for them, all of whom they did not personally train. On many occasions some of these companies would try to hire me to do the marketing for them, even though they were perceived as the marketing master. As I peered in even closer, I realized that they would learn just enough to share a result or to create a product; but in reality, they had a limited knowledge of serious marketing. This shocked me!

It also let me know that my commitment to mastery was a much bigger advantage than I had originally thought.

So I started to do things that I knew they simply couldn't do on a consistent basis, with confidence. If you want to win, you must find your competitive edge! And my edge is the fact that I control and implement all of the marketing that takes place in all of my companies. This ensures that I am generating the right type of leads that convert.

The Internet Traffic Report
One of the key things I started doing in my business to stand out in the crowd were weekly webinars that I called, My Internet Traffic Report. I would reveal the marketing platforms I was using to get leads, the amount of money I was spending on each

platform, the type of ads I was running, and I would show my back office of each marketing platform as proof!

I would even go as far as to show them how much I was earning from every webinar. I'd go on to share lots of other stats and data from my results. I wanted to make it clear that I was actually practicing what I preach.

I was determined to prove that I was the best when it came to lead generation, and I was willing to reveal the facts to prove it!

On that webinar I would purposely make statements such as, "If you are looking for a person to market your business for you and they are not willing to reveal to you what they are spending, what type of ads they are running, and their platform insights and analytics, then you may want to reconsider hiring them!"

I knew that most marketers never want to show their numbers. Because often times their numbers are not what they are claiming them to be! Or they don't resemble the screenshot they revealed on their most recent webinar or presentation!

Some people may call that cutthroat; I call it a strategic edge. Nothing was stopping them from doing the same thing I was doing; the only question was, "Could they?"

This was a way for me to prove that I was the best. And I was willing to prove it, every single week, until someone could top it.

When I started doing this, my social media websites started to explode! I got more fans on Facebook, more followers on Twitter, and more views on YouTube than all of my previous efforts, combined. I went from just being a guy who can teach marketing, which is a dime a dozen, to this renegade who walked the walk and talked the talk!

I started to get more engagement on my social media accounts than people who had 10x the fans or followers than I had.

I was always quick to point this out to my viewers. I did this to show people that you don't need a million fans and followers to get hundreds of leads per day.

Many gurus will actually buy fake fans or followers, and then use those numbers to attract clients. But when you look at the engagement on their posts or pages, they don't have hardly any.

This made my audience focus on quality over quantity, which is what I wanted them to be thinking about. And it's what I want you to be thinking about too.

The Disruption In The Industry
I started to see some marketers doing things that were out of character. For example, I would see people saying things like, "See how I generated 2000 leads in 1 day with this 1 simple method!"

Some would even do a webinar on some topic that they were not even remotely any type of expert in, all in order to try gain some momentum in their business. This is a huge mistake entrepreneurs make. I will never claim to be a blogging expert, even though I blog daily. It's not the topic that I've dedicated achieving true mastery over. Always remember to stay in your lane and do what you are great at!

Contrary to what the fake experts were trying to teach, I made it a point to let people know that it's not about how many leads you get, it's about getting the right leads and being efficient with them. This helped potential clients visualize themselves actually doing what I was teaching them.

Because when you tell a person who has never generated 1 lead in their life that they will be generating 1000's per day, they will not believe you. They will automatically think that it's not possible!

I had more people taking action than I'd ever seen before. And it's all because every week, I would fully open up my business to them. And they were able to see firsthand that it was totally possible and that they could do it too!

When I started revealing these numbers publicly, I had leaders reaching out to me and asking if I would stop revealing everything on my webinars. Some tried to do it in a nice way by sending me messages like, "Vince, be careful showing your back office. You know Facebook does not like it when you do that and it can get your account banned!"

This only proved to me even further that they had absolutely no idea what they were talking about. Because I was not running ads to these webinars. I was simply inviting my email list to them. There was a zero chance that this could get me into any trouble with Facebook.

I would reply back to them with a simple, "Thanks for the heads up."

I knew then and there that my commitment to mastery would be the advantage of a lifetime. And as long as I continued to get better and to show my results, the clients would keep coming in. So the question is... are you willing to commit to mastery? It will make all the difference for you if you do.

I also started to do a lot of live streaming on social media as well as daily videos that answered specific questions that my customers and students had. I would upload my video responses to their questions, and then I would tag them and send the videos to them.

Almost all of them would comment and thank me for taking the time to answer their questions. I knew most of my competitors would never take the time to do this.

It was my "Mark Cuban" approach to business. Meet your customers where they are at, and you will win them over forever! Remember that.

Just for those of you who are wondering what type of business owner I am. Are you curious to know whether I'm more like Trump or Cuban. It's Cuban all day long; in fact he's on the list of people I look forward to meeting one day!

The Gladiator Method
Another one of my favorite movies is Gladiator, with Russell Crowe. If you have not seen this movie, after you finish this book your assignment is to go watch it.

If you want to learn how to stand out in the crowd, this movie will provide you with the blueprint of how to do it.

In the movie, Russell Crowe plays a gladiator named Maximus who gets stripped of his power and is exiled from Rome. Then he's sent out to be killed; a command given by the son of his former Emperor.

Maximus narrowly escapes his death, but he ends up being captured and is forced to be a slave to fight to the death as a Gladiator. The slave master who owned Maximus was a former slave who also fought as a gladiator, but was set free long ago.

After winning several fights as a Gladiator in the arena, he went and asked his slave master how he could be set free. The slave master simply told him, "Win the crowd."

It's like a prizefighter who enters the ring in his opponent's hometown, but by the end of the fight, the hometown fighter's fans are rooting for the other guy. It's a classic Rocky Balboa moment!

The opponent would have to win over the crowd, and that is exactly what Maximus did.

You must do the same thing in your market. Put yourself in your customer's shoes and ask yourself, what is it that you could do to win them over? What would make you stand out from everyone else? How can you show them that you are the best?

The truth is, if you win them over, you will be on your way to earning more money than you could ever imagine. You will position yourself to add value to a lot of people's lives!

Best of all you will win the crowd just like Maximus.

"Are you not entertained?!" - Maximus Aurelius

CHAPTER 9

GRADUATE SCHOOL YEAR 3 – 3 THINGS EVERY
ENTREPRENEUR SHOULD KNOW BEFORE THEY SPEND
A SINGLE DIME ON MARKETING

Some of you may be at this point in the book, and are wondering, "Hey! Where are all of the lead generation tricks and tactics?"

"When are you going to teach me how to get leads?"

I promise you it's coming. But everything I have revealed to you thus far are things that are necessary for you to be successful *when* you start spending money on marketing.

If I don't teach you these principles first, you would've read the traffic methods, stopped reading the book, and potentially lost a lot of money only to think these strategies don't work! But your lack of results would be because you didn't learn the fundamentals first.

What I'm about to reveal to you are 3 things every entrepreneur should know about marketing before they spend a single dime.

Not knowing them will cause you to lose a lot of money, like I did when I blew $1,000 on Google Adwords when I first got started!

I also want to congratulate you for making it this far in the book. Most people would have quit by now. On most of my webinars I have what I call overtime sessions, which take place at the end of the webinar. I normally don't record the overtime sessions because I want to reward the people who attend and stay to the end!

With that being said, we are moving into the "overtime sessions" portion of the book. This is where I start to reveal to you how you can start generating leads for your business. I'll also do a bit of forecasting of where I see the future of marketing going. This will be important information to know.

But first things first. Let's talk about the 3 marketing principles every entrepreneur should know about:

The Value Of A Lead (V.O.L.)
When I first started building my business online, early on I had heard the concept of list building. The idea of building a website or a capture page to get leads. Every guru expressed the importance of building a list of subscribers to market and advertise to until the end of time.

The fact that I personally had become someone's lead, read their emails, and bought their products, made it easy for me to see that list building was something that I needed to embrace and implement into my own business!

Although I got the concept, I never understood the true value of a lead until several years into building my business.

When I ran my first ad on Google Adwords, I lost a thousand dollars so fast, thinking back I'm amazed I kept going. Losing $1,000 could have put in my head that advertising was too risky and could not be a stable revenue stream. Let's just thank God that was not the case because had I quit there is no telling what I would be doing now and you would not be reading this book.

The truth is, when you know how to advertise the right way, the *more* money you spend, the more money you will actually make. In fact, when you master it, you will often look for ways to spend more instead of doing what I did in the beginning, which is looking for ways to invest in marketing less.

The truth is, although I didn't quit, I moved forward very slowly, fearing I was losing money with every click. I lacked certainty which looking back has cost me millions!

My only other option was harassing friends and family or focusing on getting referrals!

There are some people that try to run their business and get sales from straight referrals or whatever may land in their lap.

If your business relies on referrals, in my opinion, you are not running a business. You are operating on a house of cards that will eventually collapse and crumble!

My advice is to invest in only paid advertising. This means that you are paying to get your ads displayed. This is called Pay-Per-Click (PPC) Marketing, and it's the fastest way to put a dent in your marketplace.

The first thing you will need if you are going to start generating your own leads is either a website, or a capture page, which allows you to capture a potential customer's name and email address. They give you their contact information in exchange for valuable content that you will be giving them in return.

So what is the value of a lead?

On average, every lead that you generate has a lifetime value of $1 per month to you.

So if you generate 1,000 leads, you should be earning roughly $1,000 per month. If you generate 10,000 leads, then you should be generating $10,000 per month.

This does not mean that you can't earn more with 10,000 leads. In fact, I have a company that generated over 7-figures with a little over 10,000 leads. But I also know people who have not made any money at all, and they have 100,000 leads. I will explain how this can happen later in the chapter.

When I want to know how much a person is earning per month, I can usually tell based on how many leads they have acquired.

In the last chapter of this book, there are resources that you can use to find a good autoresponder company. Autoresponders allow you to send emails and capture data on autopilot.

If you understand the true value of a lead, you will be able to position yourself to print money on demand. People who do not understand what I'm about to share with you almost always end up failing.

Let's say you have a $25 dollar per day marketing budget and you can only advertise Monday through Friday. This means that you could invest $125 per week into your business. That's $500 Per month. See the chart below:

Daily M-F $25
Weekly $125
Monthly $500

If you were to generate 10 leads per day, you would generate 50 leads per week, which would equal 200 leads per month! See the chart below:

Daily Leads 10
Weekly Leads 50
Monthly Leads 200

To determine the value of your list, you must subtract your monthly investment in leads from your monthly total of leads.

For example: If you spend $500 per month, and you generate 200 leads, the value of your asset would be -300.

Month 1 Numbers:

Monthly $$ $500
Total Leads 200
Asset Value   -300

In month two, if you invest another $500 and get 200 more leads, you are bringing your total of leads to 400. Your asset value is now -100.

Month 2 Numbers:

Monthly $$ $500
Total Leads 400
Asset Value   -100

Most people who don't realize that they are building an asset will have quit by now.

In month three, if you again invest another $500 and get 200 more leads, you are bringing your total of leads to 600. Your asset value is now +100.

Month 3 Numbers:

Monthly $$ $500
Total Leads 600
Asset Value   +100

Had I understood this early on, I would have focused on generating the right type of leads, and I would've invested into my marketing more aggressively!

Imagine if you did this for 5 years straight! You would literally position yourself to push a button and turn your computer into an ATM machine.

The point? Don't wait to start building your list. Start now! As you know, time flies. And there is no better time to do something than the present.

I remember the days where you could get clicks on page one of Google for less than 5 cents. Although, if you know what you are doing you can still get cost effective clicks with your marketing. The truth is, marketing costs are much higher than they used to be, and that's especially true for those who don't know what they are doing.

This is why you must learn to master marketing! Because if you don't, you will end up paying 10x the cost per click (cpc) than you could have been paying.

Good Leads VS Bad Leads (G.L.B.L.)

Now that you understand the value of a lead, I want to save you from a potential mousetrap that you could easily find yourself in. Especially while you're first beginning to understand this value of a lead *concept*. I also want to warn you about focusing so much on the cost per click, and even the cost per lead. What you pay per click is important, but it's not near as important as you may think, and here's why.

I get people who come to me all of the time; and all they care about is how much they are spending per click, and what it's costing them per lead.

However, what you should be focusing on is sales! Lead generation is not about getting a lead, it's about getting that lead and converting it into a sale. Leads don't pay the bills or make you rich. Sales do. 1,000 leads won't get you approved for your dream home. A load of cash will. Focus on the sales.

Learning how to get leads on the Internet just means you will have more people to talk to than your competition does. It means more people will be in front of your products and services. That is why it's so vitally important to focus on getting *targeted* leads of people who are looking for what it is that you have to offer.

If you're selling Vintage Vespa Mopeds for example, you wouldn't be targeting bearded dudes that ride Harleys. That would be a bad product to market match. You'd do much better by targeting people that have already expressed their interest in Vespa Mopeds and who are in that target demographic, which you can easily find out by doing research within that marketplace.

What is the value of a Lead Mousetrap?

When new marketers learn the concept of lead generation, and that one lead has a lifetime value of $1 per month, many of them will put all of their energy into generating as many leads as possible.

They will lose focus, and will often start generating as many leads as possible without being conscious of the *types* of leads they are generating. It's kind of like the person who tells you that they can teach you how to generate 2,000 leads per day for $50 bucks. It doesn't take a rocket scientist to know that the quality of those leads will be terrible and most likely won't convert to any sales whatsoever.

Want to know the blunt truth? If the person saying that they could generate 2,000 leads for only $50 were quality leads, most likely they would be keeping that method and those leads to themselves! Wouldn't you? A lesson to remember online and in life in general is, if it sounds too good to be true, it likely is.

Now, I'm not saying 2,000 leads a day isn't possible. I've done it, and there is a way to do it and maintain the quality of your leads.

Most importantly, the point I'm making is that I want you to remember that quality is much better than quantity. Would you rather pay $75 for 10,000 leads and get 1 sale? Or pay $200 for 1,000 quality leads and get 25 sales? Remember, it's all about the sales. Bringing home the bacon to momma.

Let me give you a few examples so you clearly understand the difference between poor quality leads and high quality leads.

I often get people who come to me and they say, "Vince, your philosophy that 1 lead has a lifetime value of $1 is not true. I have a list of 15,000 people and I've only made $600. And that was from 1 person!" After I listen to them complain about their current situation, I ask them a few questions:

"What marketing strategy did you use to build your list?" 9 out of 10 times, the following is the response I usually get.

"Well, I bought a Triple A-Rated Solo Ad!" Or, they are using some type of email scraping software that basically spams millions of people.

I will say one thing about spamming. It doesn't work! And it's a waste of your time. Don't do it!

I mentioned a solo ad in the example above. What is a solo ad? A solo ad is when you rent someone else's email list. So the list owner will email their list with your capture page link in it. They usually charge you by the click to do this. So being the desperate marketer, you are looking to build your list quickly. So you pay a solo ad provider $1,000 to email their list for 1,000 clicks. After you get your 1,000 clicks, you instantly have a list of around 400-600+ people!

What is triple-A rating? This is when the solo ad provider says that his list has been scrubbed, and it consists of only people who buy or have bought information products online.

I always laugh when they say that, because that would be like me saying my list consists of only business owners, and I focus on generating *targeted* leads.

The truth is, there is no way to 100% know what the people who opted-in to my list do or are thinking. All I can do is filter my opt-in pages to ensure I am getting the most targeted leads as I possibly can. In other words, when a local school teacher in South Carolina sees my ad in their Facebook newsfeed, and they opt-in out of curiosity, that teacher would not be in my ideal target market. Yet, she could still be on my list.

But when it comes to solo ads, it's usually people from countries that I can't even pronounce who are often on the list. And they're on the list because they were manipulated into opting-in! Maybe they were looking for furniture, and a pop-up ad appeared on their computer that says, "WIN $10,000 NOW!" The person looking for furniture says, "OK, I'll give them my email address and see what this is all about!"

Or maybe they are applying for a credit card and a pop-up ad appears that says, "Win A FREE House!" I kid you not, you would be shocked if you knew some of the things these solo ad vendors will do to build a list. And just so they can then sell them off to all of the desperate marketers out there that are looking to gamble on their marketing; instead of learning how to do it themselves, the right way. Decide and commit now to mastering lead generation the right way from the very start. Cool?

So the person that approaches me with the 15,000 leads who has only earned $600 says, "Why am I not making any sales? I spent $8,000 on these leads, nobody is buying my product, and almost none of them even open my emails." They then say the one thing that makes me fall out of my chair every time.

"I'm beginning to think this whole thing is a scam!"

This is like an overweight person walking on a treadmill while eating doughnuts, and then crying that fitness doesn't work as soon as they're not seeing the scale move in the right direction! The problem is not that it doesn't work, it's that they're not doing things right!

So I immediately ask them, "Do you ever get spam emails?" They say, "Yes, I hate spam!" At this point, they are not aware that they are basically spamming people too.

I then ask them, "Do you ever open up your spam emails?" They simply tell me, "No."

I then walk them through what they are in essence doing through the eyes of their customer. Imagine you get an email from a person you don't know, and let's just say you happen to subscribe and opt-in to their capture page.

Then, let's just say that you start getting offers to buy a product from them that you were not really looking for, nor were even remotely interested in.

What would you think of the person emailing you? This stranger? They reply to me, "I would not respect them." I then ask them if they can now see why their leads are not opening their emails. They mutter back that, yes, they can now see that's the case!

The point I'm making here is you can't cheat your way to success. There are paths that you can take that are much smoother. But there are no "push button" "skip doing the work" types of short cuts.

Your job is to find the people who want what it is that you have to offer, and then put that offer in front of them, and provide them with above and beyond value. It's a simple equation, yet, so many get it all wrong.

If you do this the right way you will build a quality list. More leads will buy from you. And you'll build a thriving business. If you focus on doing things the right way you won't mind spending more on your leads. Because you will know that they will have a much better chance of converting! Quality converts. Low quality does not.

This is why it's so important that you know the difference between "Good Leads and Bad Leads".

If you want a healthy, vibrant body? Then you'll put the best foods into it. And if you want a healthy and thriving business? You'll put the absolute highest-quality leads into it. No "junk food" leads allowed.

An Invaluable Resource – My Own Agency

There's one last thing you must master before you spend a single dime on marketing. You must become an invaluable resource to your customers.

For example, when I was doing Real Estate I was a valuable resource when the banks were lending money. The very second the banks stopped lending money, I was no longer needed.

You want to "be the bank" when it comes to your business.

That is why I chose to master lead generation. Because as long as I could generate targeted leads, I knew that my business would continue to grow.

People always ask me who handles all of my marketing, and I always tell them that I do it myself! They say, "Really!?" "Absolutely," I tell them. Driving traffic and getting leads is the lifeblood of my business. Why would I hand off something like that to someone else? Personally knowing how to attract the right customers is my edge. It's the advantage that I have over my competition. It's resulted in 7-figure profits for me.

I will outsource some things, but I will always know how to do it myself or will have a general understanding of what's going on.

When I say the term, "I am my own agency." this means that I rely on me and me alone when it comes to generating new leads and customers for my business. This allows me to never be dependent on anyone when it comes to generating revenue. I never want my ability to generate sales to be in the hands of someone else.

I know of some companies that are so focused on affiliates sales that they spend all of their time internet stalking their affiliates, making sure they are not promoting any other products but their own. This is *not* a good way to run your business.

You should view affiliate sales as bonus income, because those sales will come and go.

Why Being Your Own Agency Is Important

The American economy is much different than it was 10 or 20 years ago. The changes in the US economy have led many people to question whether or not the American Dream is alive or dead.

Can a person still work hard and get all the things they want and dream of in life?

I still believe that to be completely true. I also believe that your way of getting to the top is different though. In order to live the American Dream, you must understand (I.R.M.O.A.), which means you must be an invaluable resource, and you must be your own agency.

About 4 years ago, I had a student that I taught some marketing strategies to. This student ended up starting a company that focused on branding strategies specifically for local businesses.

My former student would handle the marketing, and her partner would handle the numbers and the bookkeeping.

When they closed the company and parted ways, my former student who handled all of the marketing picked herself up and now she earns a minimum of $1,000 per month per customer to manage business owners YouTube marketing accounts. She's crushing it!

Whereas, her partner on the other hand, was forced to figure out something else to do; and that's because she was not an invaluable resource. Bookkeepers are a dime a dozen.

The lesson to be learned here is to always position yourself to be an invaluable resource. And a good way to start it is to focus on being your own agency! Put yourself in control over the growth of your business. Never give that responsibility to others.

Why not get out a pad and pen, and do a bit of brainstorming. See how you can set yourself apart from the competition and be an absolutely invaluable resource to your customers!

CHAPTER 10

THE 5 POWERHOUSE MARKETING PLATFORMS - IT'S TIME TO GET LEADS!

I know what you're thinking. "It's about time Vince! Finally, you are going to reveal all of your lead generation secrets with me!" Well, not so fast. The next step is to break down and explain what I consider the 5 major lead generation platforms that are hot right now. Then we'll be able to progress forward to the next step in the process.

There are several ways to get leads, and there are hundreds of other platforms. Because I want to keep things simple and because I want you to be getting quality leads immediately, I am going to focus on what I consider to be the 5 powerhouse marketing platforms today.

What are the 5 platforms?

Facebook
Twitter
Instagram
YouTube
Google/Bing

I use all 5 of these platforms on a daily basis, and they are truly all you need to build a 7-figure business in any niche market that you are in.

In fact, you really only need to master one!

In my career, I have generated hundreds of thousands of leads in pretty much every type of market you could imagine. No matter what you are selling, when you have the right strategy, ask the right questions, and deliver valuable content, you will get the best leads of your life *if* you follow my exact steps as I'm about to share with you.

I will be explaining to you in detail how each platform works. You'll see how you can leverage each one to be extremely effective in your own marketing. And I'll be providing you with specific examples of what I would personally do if I were selling products in different markets; all by using these different powerhouse marketing platforms!

If for whatever reason I don't use your type of product in an example, do your best to visualize your products and how they may fit in the process. The principles and concepts we'll be discussing are universal. And they will apply to your business too. You'll soon see how a solid marketing campaign really begins before a single dime is even spent.

Before I dive into each marketing platform, I don't want you to think you have to master each method or platform at once. Focus on just 1! Then you will avoid the confusion and overwhelm that many marketers face. Remember, you don't have to know everything in just 1 day! My goal is to give you enough information so that you fully understand each platform's power. You will be able to speak about them to others with confidence. And you'll start your marketing with the knowhow to make it all work for you.

Search VS Social

Search Traffic is when a person is searching for something specific through a web browser, and an ad specific to that keyword that was searched for pops up for the consumer to see.

Social Traffic are the ads that you see on social media. You most likely were not looking for them, but they catch your eye! And the next thing you know, you have opted-in to someone's list!

It'll be important to know the difference between the two as we now move forward.

CHAPTER 11

FACEBOOK ADS - HOW THEY WORK AND THE STRATEGIES BEHIND THE ADS

How Facebook Ads Work

If you have not heard of Facebook Ads, I'm sure you have most likely seen them running rampant in your newsfeed or on the right-hand column of your Facebook page. It seems to be the #1 advertising strategy discussed amongst entrepreneurs these days. At every event I attend or speak at, there is always a Facebook guru there talking about how they have the "secret" to crushing it with Facebook Ads. Facebook Ads allows you to target people with specific interests similar to the audience demographic of who would buy your products or services. Facebook gives you the ability to run ads that will display on the right column of a person's Facebook page, to that person's newsfeed, and on that person's mobile newsfeed.

Facebook Ads are like putting a giant illuminated billboard across a busy freeway during rush hour traffic. The only difference is, that if the rush hour traffic were Facebook, you could illuminate the sign just for the male drivers, and all the vehicles that cost under $30,000. You could target just the people that you wanted to see that ad. You could target lawyers only, or only people that are obsessed with CrossFit, or only the people that are likely jamming Tony Robbins through their radios. That's power and that's the genius of Facebook ads!

The targeting power on Facebook is amazing, and it's only getting better as more and more people add more videos, content, and other details to their profiles. All of this data, along with all of the data about YOU that Facebook buys from 3rd party services, make Facebook an awesome marketing platform for entrepreneurs who choose to master it!

My View Of Facebook Ads
I do not see Facebook Ads going away any time soon. But I would be lying to you if I did not tell you that I do see the potential for millions of entrepreneur's businesses to come crashing down like a house of cards who are 100% dependent on them. This could happen for a variety of reasons. People are getting their ads accounts banned and shutdown for not adhering to Facebook's advertising guidelines. Even shady individuals who have nothing else better to do than to flag the accounts of their competitors can get your account shutdown. I've seen some of them go as far in some cases to use robots to mass flag your account. They'll execute on any and every black-hat strategy they can find to stop you from running ads.

The same thing happened a few years ago with Google Adwords. I will never forget the day back in 2010-11 when I woke up to an email from Google saying my account had been suspended. I was not affected as much as most people because believe it or not, I was running Facebook Ads way back then when most people weren't yet. I must say, I did see that coming, which is why I always leverage multiple traffic platforms. I was able to get my Google Adwords account back eventually though. I don't want you to ever have to go through this and if you have already you feel my pain. My advice for you is to master one platform at a time, yet also ensure that you do not put all of your eggs into one basket.

The coliseums of Rome that still stand to this day were not built on one pillar. They were built on many. And if one would fall, the building would not come crashing down because there were plenty of other pillars still there to hold it up. This is how you eventually want your business to be. Otherwise, you'll be putting yourself in a potentially risky situation!

Facebook Ads Strategy
Knowing all of the technical aspects of running Facebook Ads is not nearly as important as knowing how to incorporate the right strategies into your marketing. That is why I'm not going to spend too much time telling or teaching you how to set up an ad. You can easily find out how to do that by either registering for one of my 4 week Facebook Traffic classes or by simply looking at the Facebook Ads tutorial trainings inside their help desk. I'm here today to make sure you understand the core strategies behind running ads on Facebook.

Recently, Facebook has made a huge shift, as all marketing platforms eventually do in order to cater to the end user. In the case of Facebook, their end user is the person who logs-in to see what their friends are doing that night. Or the jealous girlfriend, spying on their no good man who came home a wee bit too late after a night at the bars. Or the 76-year-old Vietnam vet who is on Facebook searching for an old friend he or she served with in the military. This is what Facebook was designed for. It was not designed so that these types of people could see my ads or anyone else's ads telling them to buy a product or to become a subscriber.

The lesson I want you to remember about social media, and Facebook specifically, is that no one, and I mean NO ONE, logs-in to Facebook with the intention to buy anything.

Seriously, ask yourself when have you ever woken up out of your sleep saying to yourself, "I have to go buy that new bed, I better go log into Facebook now and buy!" It never happens right?

This means that how you approach customers must be done in a very specific and strategic way.

Most people will focus on creating the sales funnels to put their leads through when they opt-in to become a lead. On Facebook, I'm more focused on creating an *exposure funnel* by using ads before they even become a lead. If you grasp this concept that I'm about to reveal to you, more of your leads will buy from you without you ever having to sell them.

When I first start running my ads on Facebook, I'm not doing it to build a list at first. I'm doing it to build an audience so that the people I'm targeting can get an idea of what I have to offer. They are exposed to my face before I ever send them to a website or capture page.

I usually do this by creating what I call a "Value Video." This video is designed to establish credibly and authority in my marketplace.

Since you can build custom audiences on Facebook, advertisers have the ability to run ads targeting the people who have viewed your video.

When you run ads geared towards people who already know who you are, 3 things will happen:

1. You will have a higher relevance score. This is Facebook's way of grading you when it comes to how well received your ads are to the people they are displaying them to. The higher the relevance score, the more Facebook rewards you!
2. Your cost per click (CPC) will be lower. The more engaged your audience is to your ads, the cheaper your ad costs will be!
3. You will get more leads. When your audience knows, likes, and trusts you, generating leads and sales will become a lot easier.

Below is the basic format on how I run my ads on Facebook:

Step 1. Create a Value Video that breaks down your story and what it is that makes you or your products unique. Make sure you set this up to build a custom audience so you can advertise in the future to everyone who sees your video ad.

Target people who fit the interest group most likely to connect with you or buy the type of products that you have to offer. So if you sell cupcakes, don't target people who don't like carbs or are allergic to dairy. If you sell books, don't target people who hate reading. The cool thing about Facebook is that it gives you the power to filter through all of this type of data.

If you do not have a video to promote to build an audience, you could do what's called a "Like Campaign." This is when you pay to get new fans to your page. In fact, I suggest you do both a video and a "Like Campaign" to establish credibility.

> **Step 2.** Create weekly or daily content that provides value, which you can use to target the custom audience or fans and this will be the people who viewed your value video or have liked your page!

This next step will be critical to your success with Facebook: It is very important that you learn how to *include* and *exclude* people from your list when running your ads.

This way, the same people don't continue to see the same ad over and over again. Remember, people are not searching for your ads on Facebook. So if they do not know you, and they have not taken action, chances are they are not interested. This is why you would want to exclude a person from seeing your ad again after they see it or view it.

This is also why it's important to create fresh content regularly. This way, if they keep seeing your ad it will be different content every time, which will often cause them to take action out of interest versus taking action out of frustration.

> **Step 3:** Immediately run ads targeting the leads who have just opted-in, and expose them to either the video or sales letter that you are most likely going to be sending to their email address after they sign-up to your list.

The ad could say something like, "Thanks for opting-in to my list! Just in case you missed the email I sent you, click here to view the video now!"

You can do this with Facebook Retargeting by uploading your opt-in list to Facebook and then marketing to them as ads. This strategy will 10x your conversions. Seriously.

Step 4: Vary the types of ads that you run while executing Step 2. Run a video ad that leads to a website. Run straight to website ads that are clear and concise to what it is that you are offering. Send them to a page to register for a valuable webinar that you're putting on. The more you can differentiate the types of ads you are running, the more you will stand out from the crowd.

Step 5: This is the easiest part that 99% of online marketers' miss about social media. Make sure you *engage* with the people who share or comment on your content! If you can't personally do this, then have an associate to do it. Remember, Facebook is a social network. So if a person engages with you, this means they value you and will never forget the fact that you replied to them. When you do this, you are immediately exposed to all of their friends as well!

These steps are at the core of my advertising on Facebook. If you implement half of what I just shared with you, you'll have a huge advantage over your competition. And of course, you'll only get results if you start to implement these strategies. Start to put your "Action Plan" together now as you're going through these steps. Start on this right away! If you want to be success-ful, then strike the sentence "I'll do it tomorrow," from your vocabulary!

If you want to learn and master online marketing, visit: InternetTrafficFactory.com

CHAPTER 12

TWITTER ADS - HOW THEY WORK, HOW I SEE THEM,
AND THE STRATEGIES BEHIND THE ADS

How Twitter Ads Work

Twitter is a social network that allows its users to post 140-character status updates to communicate with their followers. Twitter has now made it very easy to add videos or images to your updates, which will improve the engagement you get on every status update that you post. Twitter's ad platform, in my opinion, is still very much untapped. It's made huge gains when it comes to advertisers being able to put their message in front of the people who need their products the most.

Twitter has a wide variety of ads that you can use to capture the attention of your target audience. They have also created several tools that make it fun and easy to generate leads, which they call Twitter Cards. Twitter Cards allow you to generate leads with the click of a button, allowing the customer to become a lead without ever having to enter a name or email address! What makes this feature so cool is the fact that when the person viewing the ad clicks on the Twitter Card button, the data of that user is automatically collected. Twitter will collect that person's name and email address that they used to sign-up with Twitter, thus resulting in a 100% accurate list of subscribers.

My View Of Twitter Ads

As you will soon see, there are similarities between all social networks. As you master the different marketing platforms just as I mentioned earlier in the book, you will start to see them through a different lens. Twitter has a lot of benefits that make it very different than Facebook. One of the major differences of Twitter until recently was the fact that when a status update was made, that update would automatically be placed at the top of the newsfeed of the people that are following you. This often resulted in Twitter's newsfeed looking like a giant switchboard, with thousands of messages appearing and then disappearing in seconds.

Whereas on sites like Facebook, they operate using an algorithm. Which means they only display the content that they feel you would want to see. Some gurus claim to know the secret to the algorithm by saying it's based on how often you post or engage with your audience. But the truth is, no one truly knows how these algorithms really work, and that includes me. All you can do is focus on providing the best content possible, and engaging with as many of your followers as possible.

With that being said, Twitter is changing from their free-for-all status updates newsfeed, where the most recent update is revealed immediately, to a more controlled environment like that of Facebook. Twitter has recently rolled out their new algorithm which filters the updates that they feel their users would most want to see.

INTERNET TRAFFIC & LEADS

Clearly, this is a move that will encourage advertisers to spend more to be in front of their followers. This was a huge revenue boost for Facebook when they made this change, and I'm sure it will be the same for Twitter.

I actually like this move, because it weeds out the spammers and the bad advertisers. If you have good content, then you have nothing to worry about!

Last but not least, with the new obsession with video, Livestream has become the 300 lb gorilla when it comes to authority figures reaching their audiences. Now that Twitter has merged with Periscope, when you stream live on the Periscope platform, you are also streaming live on Twitter! It only makes sense to build a huge list of followers to get yourself out in front of your target market, right?

Twitter Ads Strategy
Now let's get to the fun stuff, the strategies that will allow your Twitter advertising to result in leads and sales. When I look at Twitter, I see it as more of a branding tool than a lead generation tool. Don't get me wrong, Twitter is an amazing resource to get leads. But if you are entering a market where no one knows who you are, using Twitter the right way will get you face and brand recognition very fast.

What I love the most about Twitter is it's often managed or controlled by the actual celebrity or brand decision maker. Meaning that when you see a rant on Twitter from a major celebrity, it's not their assistant tweeting. It's really that person.

You may be wondering why that's important.

Well, if you want to win the crowd or get the attention of an authority figure in your niche, using some of the strategies I'm about to share will be a huge advantage to you.

When a person tweets about any topic, the words that they use in that specific tweet serves as a keyword that you can target when running ads through Twitter's Ad platform.

Below are a few examples:

If a person tweets, "I need a vacation NOW!"

If you had a product in the travel space, you could run an ad that appears every time a person tweets the word, Vacation.

If a person tweets, "I hate my job..."

If you are a business coach, you could run an ad that would appear in the newsfeed of every person who tweets, "I hate my job."

Can you see the power and leverage this gives you?

That is an example of the *conversations* serving as the keywords on Twitter.

Below is the basic format to how I run my ads on Twitter:

Step 1: I have a two-ad process when I start running ads on Twitter. The first thing I do is focus on building a follow campaign of people who I would consider my dream client. I target existing business owners or entrepreneurs who have products to sell, but they are not generating any leads.

I will make a list of people in my field who already have massive audiences on Twitter. I will then be able to target their audience with my ads. For example, if I wanted to target people who love personal development, then I may target the audience of Tony Robbins.

This way if they follow me, I know that when I am posting content to my followers, they are already of the right mindset of the type of people that I want to work with!

If you are into fitness, maybe you would target the people who watch the show The Biggest Loser. If you target existing entrepreneurs like me, you could target people who watch the show Shark Tank, or The Profit! No matter what you offer as a product or service, there is a person or TV show that those individuals are watching and following. If you believe in your products or services, it's your moral obligation to be in front of them, don't cha' think?!

After I make up a list of 10, I will set up a follow campaign. When a person follows you on Twitter, you can get free traffic to your websites by posting regular status updates.

The follow campaign ad may say, "Want to attract more customers using the latest marketing methods online? Follow Lead Generation Specialist, Vince Reed."

At the same time, I will run a video ad targeting that same list or audience. I do this so they can get familiar with my face and brand! This video is designed to immediately establish credibility. When a person sees this video, and then they see the other follow ad, they are much more likely to follow me.

Step 2. Send every person who follows you a direct message, thanking them for connecting with you. Again, remember this is social media. Which means a real person actually took the time to click on a button to follow you. If you or your assistant take the time to engage with them back, they will be more likely to connect with you or click on your future posts.

Here's another cool tip: when you direct message a person following you on Twitter, they will often get a notification on their phone, and in some cases depending on their Twitter settings, they may even get an email from Twitter letting them know that you messaged them. This is a powerful way to engage with your audience and stay in their mind's eye!

Step 3: Promote your latest piece of content to your followers and the custom audiences that you can also build on Twitter. This way you will never be out of sight, out of mind, with your followers.

Step 4: Promote a Twitter Lead Card to the people who view your blog posts. A Twitter Lead Card allows you to generate a lead when a person clicks the button on an ad.

Let's think about the process from the customer's perspective. When you do this you will easily see why this method works so well:

Your customers are scrolling through their Twitter feed when they see a video of you introducing yourself and establishing credibility. At this point, they have seen your face and they continue on with their day. Then they scroll the next day and they see your ad saying they should follow you. They remember they saw a video of you before, so now they are curious as to what it is that you do. So they follow you. They then get a private message from you, which they have never seen an authority figure do before, and you just made their day. If they have not hunted you down on your website and opted-in yet, you can be assured that they now know who you are. You've entered their world of awareness. A few days later, they see an ad about your latest blog post but they don't click on it. The next week, they see another ad showcasing a different post, but this time the title interests them so they click on it. They are now impressed by your ability to run ads and by the quality of your content. A few weeks later, they see a Twitter Lead Ad that says, "Click here to get 3 tips you should know about marketing on Twitter." They have *experienced* you leveraging Twitter to them, taking them from a stranger, to a face that they recognize. So they click on it, and now you have a piping hot targeted lead!

I understand that this may seem like a bit of a process, but this is how you can be effective on Twitter. This is marketing in today's economy my friend, and very few if any of your competitors are doing this. Twitter is super powerful, and if you are not using it, I encourage you to start now!

If you want to learn and master online marketing, visit InternetTrafficFactory.com

CHAPTER 13

How Instagram Ads Work

I nstagram is another social network that was purchased by Facebook. Rather than compete against Instagram, Facebook was smart enough to acquire them! Instagram Ads are managed inside of the Facebook Ads dashboard. This gives the advertiser the ability to leverage the same types of ads on Instagram as you can on Facebook.

You can run ads that once they are clicked on, it will take the person from Instagram directly to your website. Before these types of ads, it was not possible to take a person who clicked on your image to your site. The person liking your image or video would have to manually visit your website by opening up another window, and typing in your website address.

There are a few things you should know about Instagram Ads which make them different from Facebook Ads. The first notable difference is that you can only post image or video updates on Instagram. Whereas on Facebook, you can simply type out how you are feeling, and everyone knows about it without uploading an image or video. On Instagram, you have to reveal how you are feeling or what you are doing via video or an image.

The videos length has steadily increased. When Instagram started allowing video, you could only upload a 15 second video. This has since been increased to 60 seconds. This is huge for brands and advertisers, as now you have time to fully explain your message as long as you stay within the 60 second guidelines. You can't do a promoted post as of yet on Instagram, but I'm sure that will change in the future. All ads must be created within Facebook's Ad platform; and then you can run ads to that specific Instagram account. This means that people who see your ad will not see it in your list of most recent updates or pictures. For those of you familiar with a dark post on Facebook, where you run an ad that you have not posted on your page, this is essentially what you are doing when you are running ads on Instagram.

My View Of Instagram Ads

I personally think Instagram will become more powerful to the early adopters than even Facebook. The only problem is you must remain in compliance, because as of now, if you get a Facebook account banned or flagged, you are essentially getting your Instagram account banned as well!

Instagram is the new Facebook and it's where the cool kids are playing right now! What made Facebook cool in the beginning was the fact that you could only get on if you had an .EDU email address. Now that every mom and grandmother has a Facebook account, many of the original Facebook users are heading over to Instagram, and in even more extreme cases, Snapchat!

You see Facebook marketing experts everywhere, but I've yet to see anyone stake their claim as the king or queen of Instagram Ads. Opportunity is knocking, the only question is, will you beat me to it?

Instagram Ads Strategy
Advertising on Instagram became available for the general public in 2015. Making it the newest and hottest untapped marketing method today. My goal when advertising on any social media platform is to *engage* with my audience. Where most people focus on the total number of fans or followers because they view social media as a way to provide social proof to their audience, but I have a totally different perspective.

For example, some people believe it's better for them to buy fake followers and fans so that when a potential customer sees their profile, they think, "Wow, that person has 200,000 fans or followers." That can work to some extent, and I can see the logic of why some may view that as important.

Yet, what do you think happens when that person realizes their followers are fake? What do you think will happen when they see that I have 10 times the engagement with my fans, even though I may have 10 times less fans than they do?

The point I'm making is: don't worry about the number of people you have following you! Focus on the relationships you're building with each and every single one of them.

My goal when running Instagram Ads is to basically mirror everything I'm doing on Facebook. It's my chance to capture the cool kids who've left Facebook for Instagram. And it's also another way for me to stay in the sight and minds of my ideal dream customers.

Think about it from your customers' perspective; they see you on Facebook and then they see you advertising on Instagram. How many of your competitors are diversifying their marketing in this way?

Below is the basic format to how I run my ads on Instagram:

Step 1: Create a Value Video that is 30 to 60 seconds long introducing yourself, along with a call to action that instructs them to go to your website for more details.

The great thing about videos on Instagram is that once the video is complete, it will automatically repeat itself after the person sees it. Whereas on Facebook, the video will end and the screen will just go black or will show the Call-To-Action (CTA) link that leads to a website or URL. Because the videos are shorter on Instagram and because it will repeat over and over again, when it ends, it's almost like having a high powered GIF that brands you and directs your customer to where you want them to go, over and over again!

Step 2. This step is very similar to Twitter. You want to send every person who followed you a direct message, thanking him or her for connecting with you. Again, remember this is social media. Which means a real person actually took the time to click a button and follow you. If you can't do it yourself, hire someone to do it. NO Excuses here! An awesome thing with Instagram is that you can go to the profile of the person who followed you and actually send them an existing video, or image that you have already created and uploaded to your account. When you do this, they will get a notification on their phone!

Step 3: Make an image or video promoting your latest piece of content to your followers. This way, you will never be out of sight, out of mind, with your followers. This could be as simple as you grabbing your phone every week and shooting a quick video that says, "Hey, I just released my newest blog post titled: 3 Tips To Advertising On Instagram. Go to XYZ.com to gain access!"

As your Instagram following grows by using the simple video ad formula in step 1, you will begin to create a mini audience. Then you'll be able to start playing maestro! You will be able to easily direct your followers to exactly where you want them to go.

For example, let's say that you are planning to host a webinar where you are going to launch your latest product. You could simply run a video ad targeting a list of influencers' audiences in your niche, with a video ad inviting them to attend.

You could also upload that same video directly to Instagram, which would then notify all of the people following you that you are having a webinar!

My advice to you is to be where the eyeballs are. And clearly, there are millions of them on Instagram right now!

If you want to learn and master online marketing visit: InternetTrafficFactory.com

CHAPTER 14

YOUTUBE ADS - HOW THEY WORK AND
THE STRATEGIES BEHIND THE ADS

How YouTube Ads Work

N ow it's time to move into the search traffic platforms! Search Traffic is when a person is searching for something specific in a search bar, and then an ad specific to the keyword that was searched for pops up.

YouTube is owned by Google, which is a huge advantage for advertisers who use YouTube as a marketing platform of choice. Go to Google right now, and search for something specific that you feel a person would search for when they want to buy your product. There is a 90% chance that you will see a YouTube video on page 1 of Google!

I love search traffic because you get to capture what's going on inside your prospects' minds. You can truly play Houdini by placing ads that speak directly to what the person just searched for, only seconds prior.

For example, let's say that a person looking to buy a new vehicle types in, "How to get the best deals shopping for a new car."

If you were targeting people who type in "best deals new car," and you have set-up your ad correctly, there is a solid chance that your ad will display to that user.

Search traffic is great for direct response marketers because when a person is searching for something, you have the ability to deliver exactly what they want immediately. This means more leads and more sales!

YouTube Ads are managed inside of Google Adwords.

If you do not have a Google Adwords account, type in Google Adwords into Google and you can open up an account in less than 5 minutes, and it's FREE!

When creating an ad, you simply need to grab the URL of the YouTube video you want to promote, and you could be targeting people who search for specific keywords in a matter of minutes. YouTube is loaded with a bunch of advertising options. You can run placement ads, where you target people who view specific channels or videos. You can run retargeting ads, which allows you to target past viewers who have watched your videos before. YouTube has made it easy for advertisers to get their message out to the world.

There are two ad types on YouTube:
Display Ads: These are the ads that show up when people are searching, and they appear on the top or right-hand side as a related video. These are the ad types I encourage you to try out first.

In-Display Ads: These are the ads that show up before a video you are about to watch is displayed. It will force you to watch it for 5 seconds, and then the person watching has the option to skip your ad and view the original video they selected.

My View Of YouTube Ads

It's no secret that video is the future of online marketing. Recently, YouTube has added several new features. In my opinion, they've done this in order to remain relevant with video advertising, since sites like Facebook are now seriously applying the pressure! Competition is great because it adds more incredible features that advertisers can use to connect with their audiences.

YouTube has always been, and will remain to be a great resource for you to get traffic and leads for your business. But the one thing that has always made YouTube tough for advertisers was getting the person who viewed your video to actually become a lead. Most people when trying to generate a lead would use annotations on their videos in hopes that the viewer would click on the link. Some others use the bottom overlay button that you may see when you first start watching a video, which advertisers can use to try to drive traffic to their website. Recently, YouTube released YouTube Cards, which appear on the video, making it easier now to convert a viewer into a lead!

With YouTube Cards making it much easier to generate leads, coupled with the fact that you can now retarget people who view a specific video, in my opinion, YouTube still reigns supreme when it comes to video. And a lot of this is because of their connection to Google of course!

If you leverage your ads the right way, you could be getting traffic from people searching on YouTube and Google!

YouTube Ads Strategy
There are a lot of strategies that you can use to get results when it comes to advertising on YouTube. The first thing you must do is identify what type of content you are going to create, and how frequently you are going to create it.

The more videos you post, the more traffic and views you will get on your videos. The more views you get on YouTube; the more subscribers you will get as well. When people subscribe to your YouTube channel, they get notified whenever you upload new videos.

I try to release at least 1 video every single week on YouTube. Before I dive into my YouTube strategy, I have 3 tips for you to remember:

1: Keep your videos under 10 minutes, if possible.

Most people have a very short attention span, and I've found anything over 10 minutes, unless it's a webinar replay, will not hold the attention of the viewer.

2: Tell the viewer what you are going to teach them within the first 15 seconds.

Remember, when a person is searching for a video, they are looking for something specific. So if they click on your video, you want to tell them what you are going to be teaching them right away. For example, "Hello my name is Vince Reed, and in this video I'm going to reveal..." This is where you tell them exactly what they're about to watch, and then be sure to deliver on what you promised!

3: Make sure your videos always have a clear call to action.

When you are spending money on ads, you should have 2 goals. You should want to provide value first, and then you want to get a lead! I see so many people make videos, and then they fail to ask for or direct the viewer to where they need to go next to get the lead.

Your video should end by you saying something like this: "If you've received value from what you've just watched and you want to get 7 more tips on how I get leads with YouTube, then click here, or go to XYZ.com for details."

Just remember to always include a CTA. (Call to Action)

These rules sound easy, but you would be surprised by the number of people who fail to do the things I just mentioned!

Here is the basic format to how I run my ads on YouTube:

Step 1: Make a list of the keywords you want your video to target. My advice is to target the company names, or the biggest influences in your niche or space.

Step 2: Make a list of all the companies or biggest influencers in your niche market's YouTube channels or video URLs to run placement ads on. Again, this will let you run ads targeting the people who are watching your competitors' videos.

Step 3: Run a value video ad targeting the keywords and the channels, or targeting the videos of the biggest influencers in your niche.

Step 4: Run a different video that promotes your most recent content to the retargeting list of people who viewed your value video, which was mentioned in step 3

Question: Do you see a trend in my marketing style? When you are dealing with cold traffic, you can't go for the lead right away. You have to warm them up to you first.

It's like dating.

There's a process to it. You can't meet a girl on date #1, and after dinner drop down on your knees while pulling out a Diamond Ring to put on her finger. Even if you knew that "she was the one," you'd scare her off if you did that! First you need to date, get to know one another, and go through some amazing experiences together.

It's the same thing with marketing. Even if you know that it's a perfect lead for what you are selling, you have to go through the process. You can't sell right away or you'll scare them off! Let them get to know you first. Show them value. Go through some "experiences" together! And then you'll be ready to sell them. And just like falling in love, if you do this right it'll all seem to happen naturally. Selling won't be a hard thing to do!

And... that is my strategy when running ads on YouTube. Let's warm them up! If you follow this method, you will not only get more leads, but your conversions will be much higher as well!

If you want to learn and master online marketing, visit InternetTrafficFactory.com

CHAPTER 15

How Search Traffic Works

I purposely left search traffic for last because I as mentioned earlier in the book, it was the very first marketing strategy that I learned. Because of that, search traffic will always hold a special place in my heart.

When I say search traffic, I am referring to ads on either Google Adwords or Yahoo/Bing.

Although YouTube is also a search traffic website, it's solely based on videos. Whereas Google Adwords or Yahoo/Bing is not.

Search traffic ads allow you to place ads based on what a person is searching for. This is direct response marketing at the highest level!

You will be able to enter your headline, the body of the ad, and the website URL that you want to send your traffic to after they click on your ad.

No matter what a person is searching for, you will have the ability to put your ad right in front of them. Depending on what you are bidding for, a specific keyword will determine when and where your ad is shown.

Some Tips To Remember When Bidding On Keywords

There are 2 types of keywords that you have to be aware of before you start bidding.

Shopping Keywords: When I first got started advertising on Google Adwords and I lost $1,000 in less than 30 minutes, I was bidding on shopping keywords. Which are essentially people whom are simply window shopping.

An example of a shopping keyword would be a person searching for "best car to buy under $30,000" or "how to start a business". On the surface, they look like good keywords to bid on if you are selling cars or teaching people how to build a business. But the truth is, these are "shopping keywords" which means the person searching is most likely not ready to buy yet.

Buying Keywords: These are the keywords that you want to leverage when you start bidding on keywords! Had I known what I'm about to reveal to you, I would have generated leads and made sales a lot faster,

An example of a buying keyword would be "Jaguar XJL Los Angeles". This is what I personally searched for when I was ready to buy my own car. If a person is searching for that keyword, they already know what they want and are ready to buy.

What I just showed you will make a huge difference in your conversions! Knowing the difference between *shopping* keywords and *buying* keywords is critical!

You will get less traffic and clicks by focusing on buying keywords, because less people are searching whom are ready to buy right now. But if you continue to search and add relevant buying keywords to your campaigns daily, you can still get just as many clicks as if you were bidding on the shopping keywords. And the quality and conversions will be far better.

Example:

Shopping Keyword: 1 Keyword could equal 10,000 Impressions (Impressions = People Who See Your Ad)

Buying Keyword: 1 Keyword could equal (1,000 Impressions) x 10 = 10,000 Impressions.

So if you simply find more buying keywords, you can still get the same amount of traffic. And because less people are bidding on these targeted keywords, you will pay less per click!

How I Find Buying Keywords
I don't pay for any fancy keyword research tools. I simply use Google or YouTube's search bar to find my keywords. If you go

to a search engine and you start to type in a word, the most frequently searched keywords will appear. Give it a try!

For example, if you start typing the word Jaguar X... Google will display other keywords that people search for when they are typing in the word Jaguar. I use this same strategy on YouTube to get my 4 to 8 minimum recommended keywords.

My View Of Search Traffic

Search traffic will always remain a force to be reckoned with when it comes to lead generation. It stems from our human need and want for fast and immediate results.

The problem that I see with search traffic is the fact that less people are searching for solutions on Google or Bing these days. Part of the reason is because they are getting their news and updates through social media outlets. This does not mean there is no traffic to be had. In fact, because most people have left search in favor of Facebook Ads, there is a huge opportunity to take advantage of search traffic right now!

And now that search traffic websites like Yahoo/Bing are starting to display ads on Google, search traffic platforms are clearly working together to maximize the results for their customers!

Advertisers must still remember that it's all about the end user. This means when a person clicks on the ad, the pages they are taken to must be transparent. They must have privacy policies and terms and conditions on them. If you abide by these guide-lines, you will be able to generate leads on demand with search.

Search Traffic Strategies

Step 1: Make a list of 10 Core Keywords that you want to target, as well as different variations of those keywords to ensure your ads show up when people are searching for them.

Step 2: Create a capture page for each keyword to improve conversions. So if a person is searching for Jaguar XJL, your capture page headline should say "Searching For A Jaguar XJL?"

Step 3: Expand campaigns by adding 10 new keywords daily until you've reached your desired outcome of clicks and traffic.

Step 4: Place a retargeting pixel on the website that you are driving traffic to. This way, you can continue to advertise to past visitors until the end of time.

Another strategy that I encourage you to do is to target the URL's of your competitors, as well as the product names of some the products that your customers frequently purchase.

Follow these steps, and you'll be well on your way to becoming a Search Traffic Master!

If you want to learn and master online marketing, visit InternetTrafficFactory.com

CHAPTER 16

THE REAL WORLD - THE FUTURE: INSIDER TRADING AND MY 1% TARGETING SECRET OF 7-FIGURE EARNERS

I've taken you through my past, through my present, and now it's time to take you deep into the future! What a journey it's been as we have gone through the college undergraduate chapters, through the graduate school, and now it's time to go into the real world portion of this book.

What I'm about to share with you in the next few chapters is the stuff that will set you apart. It's the things that can make you a millionaire, working from anywhere in the world as long as you have a computer.

If you have read everything thus far, I want to let you know how proud I am of you. But you are not done yet! Continue reading with focus and grit as you are developing these necessary skills to your success. You're doing what the average person is not willing to do. You are finishing strong, even though you may want to put this book down and watch TV. So let's keep up the pace because you are about to read one of the most important skills of them all!

To be wealthy, you must be willing to change your habits. That's an iron-clad FACT. Bad habits are formed at an early age and have been programmed in us since birth. The key is to recognize your habits and then compare them against the habits of the ultra-successful.

Millionaires are not lucky, as some may lead you to believe. Unless you inherit your millions, earning 7-figures in a calendar year takes serious skill and effort. Let's face it, even the person who won the lottery had to get off their butt and go buy the ticket! Yet, since lottery winners rarely change their inner game and bad habits, they almost always end up losing every cent of their winnings within a few years.

If you want to earn millions, it is all about strategy really. Going a bit deeper, it's about strategic warfare! Getting your edge! And the strategic edge you will have over your competitors starts with targeting the right people. If you target the right people, you will know what they want and need before they even opt-in to your website or capture page. That is why I call this chapter of the book, Insider Trading.

If I see a man walking through the arid and dry desert when it's 110 degrees out, and I slowly drive by him in my air-conditioned car, sporting a Yeti Cooler full of ice-cold water in the backseat, what are the odds that he would want to hitch a ride with me? Pretty solid, right?

That's a good example of a good product to target market match. If he had observed me drinking a glass of hot eggnog and I had several wool blankets in the backseat, he would have had a very different response to what I had to offer him.

When you learn how to target the right people along with the secret to acquiring the right market share, you will strategically and easily position yourself to earn millions.

So the question is, how can you target the right people?

I consume 3 to 4 hours worth of content every single day. What content do I consume? I read books, I listen to audio books, I listen to podcasts, I watch training videos and any other valuable content I can get my hands on. I consume more valuable content in a day than what most people consume in an entire month!

By consuming that much content on a daily basis, I'm always learning. Which means I am in position to provide more value to the marketplace. I learned early on this powerful statement: The amount of money you earn represents the amount of value you offer to the world.

Another thing that I always tell my students is that "Your level of expectations must match your level of expertise." So if you want to earn millions but you don't have a million dollars' worth of value to offer someone, you won't become a millionaire.

The key to consuming content like I do though is that you must *execute* on what it is that you learn.

Why am I telling you this?

Well if you fail to execute on what you learn, then the information you consume is like a tree that falls deep in the forest. Nobody will ever hear that tree. It will be a useless waste of energy. And worse than that, your customer who desperately wants to learn what you have consumed will forever be lost, all because you failed to execute.

So the question is how can you quickly take information that you learn and put it into good use?

Let's look at an example:

While I was listening to a podcast late one night, someone mentioned that it only takes a 6% to 8% share of a large market to have a multi-million dollar or even billion-dollar company. They proceeded to go through the auto industry to prove their points. The point they were making was that most people think you need a huge share in the market to crush it, and you simply don't.

I took these same principles and applied them into my business whenever I'm targeting my potential customers.

How To Target The Right Customers
As I have mentioned throughout this book, you want to make a list of the biggest companies and/or influencers in your niche market. Then you want to run ads targeting the people who are already following them. You want to do this because chances are, the people following them already have interest in what it is that you have to offer.

But what I didn't share with you is that your goal is to win over 1% of each of the 10 businesses and/or influencer's audiences that you selected. If you were able to get 1% of each of the 10 that you have selected, you would have reached a 10% market share in your industry!

For example, let's say you were an opening act for a major performing artist. And let's say that artist was whomever you view as the biggest performer in the world. It could be Adele, Kendrick Lamar, U2, Kenny Chesney, or whomever else you decide to pick. Now imagine that you opened up for 9 other performers just like that person. That would mean you would have access to 10 megastars' audiences.

Now imagine you performed for the 1st big performer and 99% of the crowd hated you or were neutral about you. Not overly impressed. Yet, 1% of them LOVED you. Let's say the same thing happened at each of the other 9 performances. That would mean you would have achieved 10% market share of your audience! This is the secret to wealth, my friend. You only need to win over a small percentage of a large crowd. The key is to perform in front of as many crowds as you can with the strategic goal of capturing your 1% in each of them.

This is your goal when it comes to targeting. And it's why it is so vitally important to provide valuable content on a regular basis. The more value you provide to each audience; the better chances you have to win them over. What's another big advantage that you have? Since you can control and choose the audiences that you will target, you already have an idea of what it is that they really want!

If the performer that you were opening up for was a Rockstar, and you went out there and played Classical music, there is a very good chance that the audience wouldn't like you very much.

You may be the best classical artist in the world, but it's just not a good match for that audience. The truth is, this is exactly what most of your competitors are doing! They play classical music when their audience wants rock. They serve steak to vegetarians and vegans. They're selling basketballs to football players.

Make sure you get this right, and you'll stand apart as the clear winner.

You must know your audience better than they may even know themselves! Yet the key is, remain consistent!

Do that, and you'll get your market share, brand yourself as a leader and the money will come a lot faster.

CHAPTER 17

MY NEW CRUSH WITH SALES FUNNELS – TRIPWIRES, BETTER, BEST AND MAXIMIZER

If there was one thing I wish I would have focused on more when I first got started online, it would hands down be: Sales Funnels. I say that with a grain of salt, because I know a lot of people who spend months first trying to build a sales funnel, and they don't have a product that people actually want. And to be honest, they are so new to internet marketing they should probably be focused on selling other people's products first as they are still learning the ropes.

My lack of mastery in creating and implementing sales funnels until recently, has cost me millions of dollars. There is truly no doubt in my mind of that! I can say that with confidence as I now understand funnels at a mastery level. And when I look at what I did before, I can easily identify where I had dropped the ball. That's why in this chapter, I will reveal to you some basic sales funnel secrets that you can use to generate leads and sales. You'll be able to spend more money on advertising, even if you have a small budget. And, you'll be able to generate 10x the revenue of what you currently are earning right now.

Sales Funnel 101

Earlier in the book, I shared with you the power of a sales funnel. Your ability to filter the dirt out and only keep the diamonds. What I now want to do is give you a blueprint so that you can create a process in your business that will allow you to have financial freedom!

Most people focus all of their energy on front-end sales, which is typically the *only* thing they are trying to sell. It would be like you owning a restaurant, and only offering one item, Plain Chicken, to your customers! Uh, don't you think they may want a little bit more than just one item on the menu?!

If you have just one product, then it's not too likely that you have a sales funnel.

Let's briefly discuss exactly what a sales funnel really is: A sales funnel is basically a marketing system. It is the "ideal" process that you want your customers to experience going from prospect, to lead, to customer, to repeat buyer, then ideally a buyer into one of your high-ticket programs. And with it being a funnel, this should all be a very streamlined process!

For example: Let's say that my business is in helping soon to be brides lose those last stubborn 10 lbs so that they can fit into their dream dress, and look great on their Wedding Day.

So I go set up ads on Facebook, and target recently engaged women who have expressed interests in weight loss. Maybe they're a fan of Jillian Michael's fan page and they like Women's Health magazine and so forth. They're my prospect now. They come across my ad, and then they opt-in to get my free offer.

Now they're a lead. I add value to them and establish myself as an expert; then they eventually pick up my introductory course, Fat Loss For Brides. Now they're a buyer.

I immediately offer them an OTO (one time offer) which is a Recipe Book full of healthy and tasty meals, put together by a Master Chef who ate these exact meals to fit into her own wedding dress. Now they're a repeat buyer. I continue to follow-up and add value, and they realize they are too overwhelmed and stressed to do this all by themselves. So some of these women will invest into my high-end coaching program where they get the 1-on-1 help and customized training that they need to succeed. Now they're a high-ticket buyer. They invest in me, I deliver by making sure that they lose the weight, and they look absolutely stunning on their wedding day. A Win/Win scenario.

Now, a sales funnel can be more simple than this, or it can be *much* more complicated. This is just an example. But hopefully you get the point of what a sales funnel is now. It's pretty self-explanatory. It's a funnel that sells what you have!

When I personally create a company and start crafting my sales funnels, I like to break it up into four parts. This will provide you with further clarity on each aspect of the funnel:

Part 1: Tripwire Offer: This is a low priced, entry-level product that you can offer to provide value to your market. But it's really designed for you to get buyers. A buyer is infinitely better to have than just a lead. It is very hard to get a person to buy from you. Yet, it's easy to get a buyer that knows, likes, and trusts you to buy from you again and again. This is why you must have a tripwire offer. Make it easy and irresistible for them to buy from you on that first offer. I recommend you charging $7 – $97 on this offer!

Part 1 – Bonus One Time Offer: (OTO): Although this is a different offer, it is still part of the tripwire offer. Remember, we're taking them through a funnel. And this is the offer that appears after your customer buys, giving them a chance to get more at a discount. New on-line marketers look at this as being greedy. But the fact is, it's actually selfish if you don't offer this. If I buy something from you, and you have more that I can invest in but you don't offer it to me? Then you are preventing me from getting what I need as a consumer. This OTO offer is often what will pay for your marketing expenses as well! When you start getting 1 or 2 of your customers to buy your One Time Offers, you will be able to spend more on advertising, and a lot faster.

Part 2: Better: This is the 1st level product upgrade that you can offer to your customers. This product should provide more value and should be 10x the price of your tripwire offer at a minimum. I try to keep this product between $297 and $997.

Part 3: Best: This is when you start to get into your higher ticket products and services. These are the products that will push a 6-figure earner into the 7-figure category. The products must make sense to the offer, and they should be priced in the $1997- $9,997 range!

Part 4: Maximizer: The maximizer is your highest priced product that you have to offer. It's your Mercedes Benz offer. You will not sell a lot of maximizers per month because they are for your top clients. The price point should not only make your customer uncomfortable, but they should make you uncomfortable as well. This will bring out the best in you and your clients. The price points should be $19,997 – $99,000. If you don't feel that you could charge fees like that, then you have to improve your personal value levels, my friend! Ask yourself, if Warren Buffet charged $19,997 for mentorship, would it be worth it? Heck yes, it would be robbery... it would be a steal!

And what's great is that you'll find out that the higher you charge, the higher the success rates of your customers will be. Somebody may or may not be motivated to act on something they learned from a $7 product. There's not much to lose in the "loss ratio" there. But when they've invested $7K? They've got some skin in the game now buddy! And they will be much more likely to do something with it and it can change their lives.

So, you're providing true value here as your customers ascend up the price and value ladder.

If you have an existing company or if you are getting ready to start one, ask yourself what are your tripwires, one-time offers, and your better, best, and maximizer products? If you do not have your business set up this way, I want you to go to a whiteboard and write down a process using your products. If you don't have a whiteboard, then write it out with a pad and pen.

It's super important for you to see how this works from a visual perspective! Last but not least, don't focus on the price points as much as in the *thought process* on how you are going to structure your products.

This basic set-up is what I use with every business I run. The last part of the puzzle is for you to get a sales team to offer your backend products to your customers! A good phone team is what's going to set your business apart! The faster you implement them into your business, the quicker you will be waking up to big commissions!

Ignore all of this advice at your own Peril!

CHAPTER 18

INTERNET TRAFFIC FACTORY - FACTORY MASTERMIND

As I write this book, I am preparing to launch my newest company: **Internet Traffic Factory.**

It was probably not smart to write a book in one week at the same time I was launching a company; but I love pressure! Pressure makes diamonds. And I seem to get my best work done when I set crazy deadlines for myself.

My new company, Internet Traffic Factory focuses on helping customers actually implement the strategies that I teach. It's almost like an online University where people can enroll in online marketing workshops that last from 2 to 4 weeks. They are 100% focused on 1 marketing platform at a time. Let's say you want to master Facebook marketing. You could enroll in our Facebook workshop and learn how to set up ads that convert for your own business. By the end of the workshop you will have the skills to generate quality leads and have the skill set to teach what you learned to others!

I love lead generation strategies, but the truth is, the methods I teach change frequently. Which is why I decided that

Internet Traffic Factory *must* be created. So instead of buying a product with several modules, and hours of content that can quickly become outdated our workshops are live and reveal what's working and happening now in real time.

As I continue to write this book I have been going back and forth on how detailed I wanted to go when it comes to me revealing my new company's business model. But I figure if you are still reading this, you are serious about your success and I want to leave no doubt that I'm here to serve you. With at being said, you are about to go deep inside my business.

I read a lot of books, but I am yet to read a book where the author reveals their exact business model. What you normally get is good content on basic theories, as to how you can build a business. So like always, I wanted to separate myself from the pack by breaking down my funnel, giving you real world examples so that you never have to guess when it comes to you building your business. What you will learn next is exactly how I implemented the tripwire offer in my new company, all the way up to my maximizer product offers. Let's dig in!

Also, know that things change so what I reveal to you now is always subject to change.

The Internet Traffic Factory Business Model
Our entry level product is called our Factory Mastermind. It consists of a 4 week coaching program and several lead generation training modules guaranteed to help you get more traffic and leads for your business. Clients get weekly coaching

sessions and access to a private group to get all of their questions answered.

Once a person purchases that product, they are offered a one-time offer (OTO) where I teach them how I personally create sales funnels. Your OTO should make sense, but it should not be more of the same things that were offered in the first product.

For example, the tripwire offer is teaching traffic and lead generation strategies. So it only makes sense to teach people who buy that product how to create sales funnels, as to ensure that the leads that they are generating converts! So the offer is not the same, yet they complement each other perfectly.

Internet Traffic Factory is 100% focused on helping clients *execute* what I teach them. So our "BETTER" product is an offer that allows the customer to enroll in online marketing classes. We call these products online workshops and they can range from 2 to 4 weeks long. The classes focus on different marketing strategies every month. So if you want to learn Twitter, Facebook, YouTube or any other topic all you have to do is enroll and get up to date real time training.

Why do I do this?

It's the same reason your car keeps track of how many miles you have driven. After a while your car will run it's course and you will have to buy a new one. Although most entrepreneurs don't want to hear it, marketing methods change frequently. Traffic strategies change daily so by doing online classes focused on 1 topic, it allows me to keep the content fresh and current while allowing our clients to purchase a brand new shiny car... or enroll in another class after they've racked up the miles on the strategies from a different marketing concept.

After a customer starts to get results by mastering a specific method, the next step is to provide them with other products and services that allows us to help them with their specific business needs. Things like done for you sales funnels, creating webinar presentations for them, video branding packages and more. This would be considered a "BEST" product.

As customers progress, there will be a handful of them that will see the value in having a full mentorship relationship with me. This is why we provide extended coaching packages, live events and even destination events in tropical locations. These would be considered our "MAXIMIZER" products.

Last but not least be sure to hire some skilled phone sales reps to follow up with your leads. No matter how good you get at lead generation nothing beats a real live person providing quality 1 on 1 coaching and training!

That's it... A simple but powerful funnel, right?!

But remember, you can have the best funnel or business model in the world but it won't work unless you feed the business with good quality leads.

This book will serve as a key role in helping me generate targeted leads for my business along with all of the key marketing strategies I've shared as well.

Now that I have broken down my business model to you, there are two things you need to do. The first thing you must do is map out the process you want to take your leads through. Yep, you need to map out your own funnel. This should be an exciting and fun process for you to go through!

And then, the second thing you'll want to do is to actually start sending targeted traffic through that funnel!

If you need help, Internet Traffic Factory is here to help you.

It's almost time for you to execute what you have been learning throughout this book!

One more chapter to go...

It's time to finish strong!

CHAPTER 19

The Humble Yourself Story

As I start to write this last chapter, I can't help but to feel extremely proud of myself. I know I put my heart and soul into it, and I hope you take what you have learned and use it to make an impact in the world. Both to your world, and to that of many others.

I know this book was probably not what you were expecting. There were a lot of stories and real life events that I hope you learned from. But before I let you go, I have a few more stories for you. I call this my "humble yourself "story.

One of the biggest lessons I ever learned was that you don't know what you don't know. Ya know?! Another lesson that always sticks with me is to aim to extract value from everything! That means when you are bored and you feel like you are not getting any value, that is when you should focus even more, because that is when you often find the gold!

For example: Years ago, I attended a FREE marketing event hosted by Mitch Meyerson, who co-authored the book, Guerrilla

Marketing On the Internet. This was when my head was starting to get a little too big, because I was starting to earn commissions on a consistent basis in my business.

There were probably 300 to 500 people in the audience. I was sitting in the back of the room, and I remember there was a speaker on stage who was talking about how much money they were making, and they kept asking the audience questions.

Let's go back to that room…

Speaker: Raise your hand if you want to earn more money in a day than most people earn in a month.

Me: I don't raise my hand.

Speaker: If you want to be on stage one day sharing your story with the world, raise your hand?

Me: I don't raise my hand.

Speaker: If you are sitting there and you did not raise your hand, that means 1 of 2 things. You are full of yourself and feel too cool for school… And the truth is no one is looking at you, they are all looking at *me*.

Or, you are not open enough to make the changes needed to achieve the goals I know you want to achieve… If you can't bring yourself to raise your hand, what are you going to do when things really get tough?

Me: Ouch… (What I was thinking?!) He is absolutely right. You've been raised to be a leader, not a follower. Humble yourself you jerk! (Today, I'm humble and proud of it!)

From that moment on, I made it a point to get comfortable with being uncomfortable. I made the decision to always remain the student, and to listen intently to what others have to say. Most people are too proud to listen, and the second they have success, they feel they have all of the answers.

At that very moment, after I realized that I was acting like a complete idiot at that event, I tuned-in and picked up several golden nuggets that I still use to this day. In fact, I remember that I was going to leave early, but then I decided to stay. And because I did, I was there when they passed out this awesome resource guide that I will use forever. Had I left, I would have never known that some of those resources even existed!

Entrepreneurs are the ones who make the world go around! We are the people that innovate and inspire people to take their business to the next level. The more we open up our businesses and our lives, the more we can all learn from each other. I hope this book inspired you and let you know that you can accomplish anything you put your mind to.

I hope you got a ton of value here. And until next time, I will see you on the internet! As I mentioned earlier, online traffic and marketing can change on a daily basis. To stay on the cusp and cutting-edge of what's working now, I encourage you to head on over and check out my site at: **InternetTrafficFactory.com**

I sincerely hope I can be your trusted advisor and partner on your journey to millions.

Now get out there and execute.

Your Friend And Online Mentor,

Vince Reed